Faith and the Political in the Post-Secular Age

In the emerging post-secular environment, how might the wisdom and prophetic power of Christian faith make its particular contribution? This superb collection of erudite, accessible and theologically insightful essays offers fresh and sharp perspectives on politics and faith for today. An engaging and richly rewarding ecumenical book, that presents a shared Christian message of hope as an antidote to contemporary cultural (political) scepticism. The book will be of interest to all who seek to engage, within the context of local and global political debate, in a cogent and coherent vision of the common good.
Bishop Stephen Pickard
Professor & Executive Director, Australian Centre for Christianity and Culture, Charles Sturt University.

Jesus Christ challenged with prophetic passion and compassion the oppressive cultures of his day. So do the authors of this remarkable book. Having analysed with professional skill critical issues in our own cultures, they show they can be transformed through gospel values. This is public theology at its best!
Dr Gerald A. Arbuckle, SM
Co-director, Refounding and Pastoral Development, Sydney

Faith and the Political in the Post-Secular Age is the second of three books in the series, *Explorations in Practical Theology*. This book offers a critique of diverse forms of fundamentalism and faith in the post-secular context. The breadth and depth of research of the contributors across the spectrum of public theology in the Australian context present the reader with key secular and ecclesial challenges that are foundational to those searching for faith and meaning in their lives.

Those working in the academy or in ministry will find a resource which is addressed to the Australian context and to the social and political questions of the time. Coventry Press, under the auspices of the series editor, Anthony Maher, has enabled readers to taste the fruit of scholarly research in a dialogical community context.

Professor Maryanne Confoy RSC
Jesuit Theological College / University of Divinity

Faith and the Political in the Post-Secular Age, edited by Anthony Maher, adds significantly to the growing store of research applications in the field of practical theology, offering a collection that demonstrates well the relevance of theological reflection to contemporary events in the public square. In that sense, the collection confounds the populist view that theology as a discipline belongs to an age gone by and has nothing to offer to today's post-religious world. The chapters in this book show clearly why this is not the case; be it about political economy, social welfare or post-secularity in general, applying a theological lens is an important adjunct to any other disciplinary probe. This is at the heart of the field of practical theology and this book's contents provide a grand example of the unique insights that it can elicit.

Dr Terence Lovat, Emeritus Professor, The University of Newcastle, NSW

EXPLORATIONS IN PRACTICAL THEOLOGY

FAITH AND THE POLITICAL IN THE POST-SECULAR AGE

ANTHONY MAHER, EDITOR

COVENTRY
PRESS

Published in Australia by
Coventry Press
33 Scoresby Road
Bayswater Vic. 3153
Australia

ISBN 9780648230311

Compilation copyright © Anthony Maher, editor, on behalf of APTO, 2018

The copyright of individual chapters remains with the authors of those chapters.

All rights reserved. Other than for the purposes and subject to the conditions prescribed under the *Copyright Act*, no part of this publication may be reproduced, stored in a retrieval system, or transmitted in any form or by any means, electronic, mechanical, photocopying, recording or otherwise, without the prior permission of the publisher.

Cataloguing-in-Publication entry is available from the National Library of Australia
http:/catalogue.nla.gov.au/.

Text design by Filmshot Graphics (FSG)
Cover design by Ian James – www.jgd.com.au

Printed in Australia

Contents

Acknowledgments 8

Contributors 9

Introduction
Anthony Maher 12

Chapter One: Fundamentalisms and the Emergence of the Post-Secular Age
Anthony Maher 21

Chapter Two: Post-secularity
Elaine Graham 50

Chapter Three: 'Post-secularity and Australian Catholics'
Bob Dixon 72

Chapter Four: Towards a Practical Political Theology: A Provisional Typology of Public Faith in a Post-Secular Age
Andrew Cameron 92

Chapter Five: Faith and the Political: Former Prime Minister Tony Abbott
John Warhurst 110

Chapter Six: Emmanuel Levinas: Society, Justice and Mercy
Terry A. Veling 122

Chapter Seven: The Emerging Approach to Political Economy of Pope Francis
Brendan Long 134

Chapter Eight: Discerning the Place for the Prophetic Voice and Pragmatic Co-operation of the Churches in the Great Moral Questions of the Age
Frank Brennan 156

Dedication

To Neil Darragh

New Zealand Priest, Practical Theologian and Fellow of APTO

Acknowledgements

This book is a collective effort of practical theologians engaging faith and the political, whilst testing the post-secular hypothesis. The book would not be possible without the generosity of colleagues delivering a keynote paper to the APTO annual conference and writing the subsequent chapter now presented in this collection. Particular thanks are warranted for the critical review by Gerard A. Arbuckle and the sterling support of Zach Duke, Bob Dixon, Merv Soares (LMent Graphic Design)and Hugh McGinlay of Coventry Press.

Contributors

Frank Brennan
Frank Brennan is a Jesuit priest and CEO of Catholic Social Services Australia. He has been professor of law at Australian Catholic University and Adjunct Professor at the Australian Centre for Christianity and Culture, the Australian National University College of Law and the National Centre for Indigenous Studies. An Officer of the Order of Australia (AO) for services to Aboriginal Australians, he was the recipient of the Migration Institute of Australia's 2013 Distinguished Service to Immigration Award and of the 2015 Eureka Democracy Award in recognition of his endeavours which have contributed to strengthening democratic traditions in Australia. The National Trust has classified him as a Living National Treasure. His research interests include conscience and faith, human rights and the rule of law, and the rights of Indigenous peoples and asylum seekers. His latest books are *No Small Change: The Road to Recognition for Indigenous Australia*, *Amplifying That Still, Small Voice*, *The People's Quest for Leadership in Church and State* and *The 2015 Gasson Lectures: Maintaining a Convinced and Pondered Trust*.

Andrew Cameron
Revd Dr Andrew Cameron is the Director of St Mark's National Theological Centre in Canberra, and an Associate Professor in the School of Theology at Charles Sturt University. He is a member of the Public Affairs Commission of the General Synod of the Anglican Church of Australia, and has held other lectureships and posts in ethics and moral theology. His research interests include the relationship between ethics and emotion, and he has authored Joined-up Life: A Christian Account of How Ethics Works (Nottingham: IVP, 2011) and Living in the Next Phase: Developing the Theology, Practice and Ministries of Later Life (Sydney: Anglican Deaconess Ministries Limited, 2014).

Robert Dixon
Robert Dixon was the Foundation Director of the Australian Catholic Bishops Conference Pastoral Research Office from 1996 to 2016. He has a PhD in sociology from Monash University as well as degrees in science, theology and education. He is an Honorary Professor of Australian Catholic University and an Honorary Research Fellow of the University of Divinity where he serves as a member of the university's Research Committee. The author of *The Catholic community in Australia* (2005), he is also the author or co-author of numerous other books, book chapters, journal articles and reports about the demography of the Australian Catholic population and about aspects of Catholic belief and practice. His most recent publications are 'The Demography of Australia's

Catholics: Method and Applications' in the *Yearbook of International Religious Demography 2017* (Brill) and as lead author of *Our Work Matters: Catholic Church Employers and Employees in Australia* (Australian Catholic Bishops Conference).

Elaine Graham

Elaine Graham is the Grosvenor Research Professor at the University of Chester, UK and Canon Theologian of Chester Cathedral. She is the author of *Making the Difference: Gender, Personhood and Theology* (1995); *Transforming Practice: Pastoral Theology in an Age of Uncertainty* (1996), *Representations of the Post/Human: Monsters, Aliens and Others in Popular Culture* (2002) and *Words Made Flesh: Writings in Pastoral and Practical Theology* (2009). She is co-author, with Heather Walton and Frances Ward, of *Theological Reflection: Methods* (2005) and, with Stephen Lowe, of *What Makes a Good City? Public Theology and the Urban Church* (2009). Her two most recent books have focused on the role of religion in a pluralist, secular society and the possibilities of a more 'apologetic' dimension to Christian public engagement: *Between a Rock and a Hard Place: Public Theology in a Post-Secular Age* (SCM, 2013) and *Apologetics without Apology: Speaking of God in a world troubled by religion* (Cascade, 2017).

Brendan Long

Brendan Long is a Senior Research Fellow at the Australian Centre for Christianity and Culture, which is a research institute of Charles Sturt University in Canberra, Australia. He is an economist and theologian with a Ph.D. from the University of Cambridge on the religious aspects of the thought of Adam Smith. He has published articles in international journals in this area *(Adam Smith Review and Edward Elgar Companion to Adam Smith)*. His current research focuses on connections between economics and theology. Recent publications have involved analysis of a Christian ethical approach to tax policy reform in Australia, and he was the quest editor of a Volume of the *St Marks Review* devoted to this issue. He has also been a senior political adviser to four Cabinet Ministers.

Anthony Maher

Professor Anthony M. Maher is a Research Fellow of the Centre for Public and Contextual Theology at Charles Sturt University, Australia. He is the series editor of two ongoing projects: (i) *Explorations in Practical Theology* and (ii) *Educating Hearts: Ignatian Characteristics for formation and Education*. He is currently working on a *George Tyrrell Reader*, a compilation of ten seminal essays by George Tyrrell. His most recent book is *The Forgotten Jesuit of Catholic Modernism*, (Augsburg Fortress, 2018).

Terry Veling

Terry A. Veling teaches at St Paul's Theological College, Australian Catholic University, Brisbane. He also taught for many years in the United States and was a Golda Meir Fellow at the Hebrew University of Jerusalem. He is the author of Practical Theology (Orbis, 2005) and most recently, *For You Alone: Emmanuel Levinas and the Answerable Life* (Cascade, 2014).

John Warhurst

John Warhurst AO is an Emeritus Professor of Political Science at the Australian National University in Canberra where he was Professor of Political Science from 1993-2008. He is a specialist lecturer and writer on religion and politics and this chapter grew out of work undertaken when he was a Research Fellow on "The Faith of Australian Prime Ministers" in the Australian Prime Minister's Centre at the Museum of Australian Democracy, Canberra. His PhD was from the Flinders University of South Australia and he is a former president of the Australian Political Studies Association.

Introduction

Anthony Maher

A Work of Public Theology

Our time is experiencing a resurgence of religious consciousness which leads some scholars to posit a post-secular hypothesis. The purpose of the current book is to explore this post-secular proposition, whilst articulating a practical theology that is responsive to the public square.[1] This is the second publication in the Explorations in Practical Theology series, the third book is currently in process, Engaging the Politics of Division, and will be published in the second half of 2018.

Public theology is predisposed to a consequential commitment to the common good. Such preference requires interaction with economics, media, politics, law, globalisation, social justice and the environment.[2] Public theology addresses the moral and social concerns not just of individuals, but of structures and systems of power within governments, corporations and ecclesial institutions.[3] Principally, public theology seeks to offer a religious and spiritual contribution to the political space and engage in transparent and publicly accessible dialogue with those beyond the immediate faith community. Public theologians and theologians who do theology in the public square are challenged to "speak truth to power", growing out of specific religious traditions they strive to be engaged in the concrete reality of ordinary life, as they seek to 'give reason to the hope that is within them' (1 Peter 3:15).[4]

---

[1] Each chapter in this work began life as a keynote paper presented to the annual conference of the Association of Practical Theology in Oceania (APTO), held at the Australian National University in Canberra, November 2015.
[2] Max Stackhouse, *God and Globalisation, Volume 4: Globalisation and Grace* (New York: Continuum, 2007); E. Harold Breitenberg Jr., 'To tell the truth: will the real public theology stand up?' *Journal of Society of Christian Ethics* 23.2 (2003): 55-96; Elaine Graham and Stephen Lowe, *What Makes a Good City? Public Theology and the Urban Church* (London: SPCK, 2009). Elaine Graham, *Between a Rock and a Hard Place: Public Theology in a Post-Secular Age*, (London: SCM Press, 2013), 22.
[3] Breitenberg, 'To Tell the Truth'. Graham, *Between a Rock and a Hard Place*, 22.
[4] Elaine Graham, Chapter Two above, and Avery Dulles, *A History of Apologetics* (First published 1971). (Eugene, ON: Wipf and Stock, 1999), xix.

Faith and the Political in the Post-Secular Age

Jürgen Habermas optimistically understands the emerging post-secular hypothesis as 'a hope in God as the grounding for pragmatic moral action, providing inspirational visions of human solidarity.'[5] In testing the post-secular hypothesis, **Anthony Maher** in Chapter One denotes the developing context of the secular age and critiques three prevalent examples of closed-truth fundamentalist notions of 'ultimate reality': (i) religious fundamentalism, (ii) proselytising atheism, and (iii) uncompromising neo-liberalism. The chapter moves on to test the above three virulent responses to the question of post-modern insecurity before concluding with a prolegomenon to a fourth evolving pathway. The fourth pathway seeks to be a relevant response to post-modern insecurity and involves a diachronic and synchronic *modus operandi*. One cognisant of a chastened Christianity, modelled upon the humble servant of Isaiah, a liberated and 'refounding' Christianity situated at the crossroads of post-modernity.

Drawing upon the work of Habermas in Chapter Two, **Elaine Graham** asks: how does the church, 'speak Christian into this strange new world, both fascinated and troubled by religion?'[6] Graham highlights the assumption of classical secularisation theory with regard to the steady decline of religion in western post-industrial societies and the paradoxical often disturbing resurgence of religion. There is, Graham explains, a contemporary situation which fits neither a narrative of secularisation nor one of religious restoration. Graham considers 'this unprecedented, unanticipated, agnostic co-existence of religion and secularism is sometimes termed the "post-secular"'. Graham suggests we think of ourselves as occupying a new space, somewhere between the renewed visibility of religion in public life, with its (somewhat reluctant) recognition of the importance of religious values and actors on the one hand, and the persistence of widespread scepticism towards religion on the other, with its enduring

---

[5] Graham, *Between A Rock and a Hard Place*, 45.
[6] James Haire described Graham's book *Between a Rock and a Hard Place* as recasting 'the whole Christian enterprise in the public context of post-secular societies internationally. She thus reinterprets Christian apologetics, and indeed Christian existence, in the multi-religious context of the global community. For anyone concerned with the church's future this is a seminal study.' James Haire, Elaine Graham, *Between A Rock and a Hard Place*, (2013).

expressions of secular objections to religion as a source of legitimate public discourse.

Reminiscent of C.S. Lewis' intention, Graham is concerned to offer a Christian apologetic for our time and context. She believes a possible response to the current ambiguity around secular theory and the rise of religious fundamentalism is 'a restoration of traditions of public theology towards a kind of Christian apologetic'. Indeed, Christianity is once again, as on many occasions though history, called upon to offer in the public space, in the full light of human achievement and endeavour, a reasoned defence or rationale both in word and deed for the Christian faith. Graham describes this praxis in the public space as 'an invitation to inhabit a shared space of dialogue and exchange in the spirit of hospitality'.

Public theologians then are continuously challenged in an ecclesial and secular context to critique hegemonic interest. Inspired by faith in the Gospel and understood as a central imperative, public theologians seek to mediate insights and truths from the Gospel and tradition into the public market place of ideas. Graham convincing argues that we might best understand Christian apologetics not so much as competition or seeking empirical truth but rather more as a way of life, a way of being, offering practical evidence that is performative witness rather than combative philosophical proposition.

In Chapter Three, **Bob Dixon** offers a seminal consideration of 'Australian Catholics' as a case study for the post-secular hypothesis. Through analysis of twelve key features of the contemporary Catholic community, informed by sociological research, Dixon tests the supposed failure of the secularisation thesis and suggests 'that it is more helpful to think of post-secularity as a consciousness that develops within a secular society'. In a personal reflection that is essential reading for all those interested in the future of the Catholic Church in Australia, Dixon questions to what extent can the term 'post-secular' be applied to Australian Catholics, and how does it help us understand contemporary Catholicism and the challenges it faces.

Dixon critiques three elements of post-secularity: resurgence of religion, a willingness of secular society to engage constructively with the ongoing phenomenon of religion, and finally, religious and spiritual diversity. In reviewing this chapter, one of the world's seminal contributors to the sociology of religion, José Casanova, described Dixon's work as 'a magistral analysis of empirical trends' and 'a very nuanced correct evaluation of the Australian situation in terms of the debates concerning secular and post-secular societies'.[7] Casanova highlighted that Dixon presents an 'insightful diagnosis of the disjunction of the church and the world or secular society, in terms of the two different moral compasses of "human rights" and traditional "natural law"'. Casanova argues that, 'the church needs to recognise that what is stake is not modern moral anomie or degeneration (paganism), but rather a fundamental conflict between two different universalist principles of morality.'

Andrew Cameron in Chapter Four articulates a provisional typology of public faith in a post-secular age through the prism of Christian political ethics. His purpose is to help us navigate the political dynamic less committed to grand theory and disputes, and more able to move practically into the world - albeit well-informed by political theology, by our faith gone public, and by a canny awareness of the shifting canons in our secular or increasingly post-secular culture.

Cameron reasons that we do not, and probably cannot, make global decisions about what theory to use for every political question; 'but that we can and do have the Christian wit and wisdom to consider creatively some political candidate approaches to this or that political issue or question'. In appropriating some of the core insights of Christian ethics today, Cameron highlights how taking this creative approach would help to diffuse the inter-Christian disputes that are engendered when we insist that we have to have one theory and approach before we engage in politics. In essence, internal denominational wrangling diverts theological resources, saps energy and evaporates good will, while creating a religious vacuum in the public square which is increasingly occupied by polarised divisive and simplistic reaction to complex contemporary social events. In reviewing chapter four, Brian Brock commented that Cameron is encouraging us 'to think about politics that is not so committed to theory that we have to fight about

---

[7] José Casanova is a Professor at the Department of Sociology at Georgetown University, and heads the Berkley Center's Program on Globalisation, Religion and the Secular.

theory before thinking about important political questions. These are worthy thoughts and timely ones as well.'[8]

In Chapter Five the seasoned political commentator **John Warhurst** identifies the former Prime Minister Tony Abbott, described as 'Captain Catholic', as an obvious case study of faith and the political within the post-secular age. The former Prime Minister is so identified with the Catholic/Christian faith that in many respects he may well have benefited from the typology outlined by Andrew Cameron in the previous chapter. Indeed it may well have prolonged his time as Prime Minister. Tony Abbott resolutely rejects the secular dictate that understands religion to be a private affair. He was one of the most combative and divisive Prime Ministers in living memory.

Warhurst's nuanced study grows out from his research into the faith of Australian Prime Ministers (for the National Museum, Canberra), to determine how their faith intersected with politics. Warhurst offers a portrait of Abbott that is highly relevant and stimulating to our broader discussion of faith and the political. Warhurst shows that having a strong public religious identity leaves one prone to intense media ridicule. Abbott was cruelly vilified as the 'mad monk', even so, and, unlike in the United Kingdom, his faith did not preclude him from the highest office in Australia.[9] Indeed one could argue that a strong Catholic faith leads many into a life of public service for the common good, although the extent to which that faith influences public policy is uncertain and still requires further critical analysis.

In Chapter Six, **Terry Veling** illustrates with exceptional proficiency the application of the thought of Emmanuel Levinas to our question of 'faith and the political'. As an acknowledged international expert on Levinas, we are in debt to Veling for allowing a wider readership access to one of the most profound Jewish thinkers of the twentieth century.[10] Here Veling enables us to appreciate that Levinas' 'ethic is at once an intellectual edifice and an extended prayer'. Inspired by Levinas' face-to-face ethical relation of being for the other, relevant

---

[8] Dr Brian Brock, Reader in Moral and Practical Theology, Department of Divinity, History and Philosophy, King's College, Aberdeen.
[9] The United Kingdom's unwritten constitution makes it "awkward" for a Catholic to become Prime-Minister and the 1701 *Act of Settlement* prohibits 'papists' from inhering the throne.
[10] Terry A. Veling, *For You Alone: Emmanuel Levinas and the Answerable Life*, (Eugene, Oregon: Cascade Books, 2014).

to our own Trump era, Veling warns of the dangers implicit in social-political systems and institutions becoming self-serving rather than serving the people they were created for: universities for students, hospitals for patients, governments for people and so on.

Veling articulates an ethical imperative for public theology and the engagement of faith in the political space. Suspicious of all philosophical systems and ideologies, Levinas teaches that the charity of one-for-the-Other is never completely fulfilled by public justice or any social political system. 'Politics left to itself bears a tyranny within itself.' Offering a masterful critique of the political and the administrative, Levinas laments, 'Oh the violence of administration... which sees law and politics turned into an idol.' Levinas urges us to be one-for-the-Other, to carry each other, to be for each other, to escape the narrow confines of our small egoism. According to Levinas, this turning towards the other, this face-to-face is the essential divine and ethical relation. God in the other is not a metaphor. Levinas insists in the other there is real presence of God. 'The other is not God, but in his or her face I hear the word of God'.

In highlighting the prophetic work of Levinas, Veling challenges us to consider closely the inherent risks associated with the faith-political synthesis. Veling asks what sort of policies would we promote or what kind of actions would we take if we were to speak of social mercy as resolutely as we speak of social justice?[11] In announcing the "Year of Mercy" (Dec. 2015-Nov. 2016), Pope Francis hoped to focus world attention on the plight of the poor and marginalised.[12] While much of the Church's focus and energy has been on internal interpretation of particular doctrine around marriage and sexual ethics, arguably, the Pope is attempting to draw attention to global inequality.

---

[11] Terry A. Veling, *The Beatitude of Mercy: Love Watches Over Justice* (Eugene, Oregon: Wipf and Stock Publishers, 2015).

[12] Pope Francis writes: "It is my burning desire *that, during this Jubilee, the Christian people may reflect on the corporal and spiritual works of mercy. It will be a way to reawaken our conscience, too often grown dull in the face of poverty. And let us enter more deeply into the heart of the Gospel where the poor have a special experience of God's mercy. Jesus introduces us to these works of mercy in his preaching so that we can know whether or not we are living as his disciples" (Misericordiae Vultus,* 15). The seven corporal *works of mercy: to feed the hungry; give drink to the thirsty; clothe the naked; welcome the stranger; heal the sick; visit the imprisoned; bury the dead.*

Brendan Long in Chapter Seven outlines Pope Francis' emerging approach to political economy, in the process shedding light on one of the most significant merges of faith and the political in the secular age. Pope Francis is a major world figure and perhaps the most significant exemplar of the post-secular hypothesis. Francis moves spontaneously back and forth across spiritual and political boundaries, drawing upon the Gospel and Ignatian spirituality to comment upon social and political events in the public square. Long utilises his considerable political experience to analyse Francis' political sortie. He characterises Francis' emerging approach to political economy as 'reflective praxis', through engagement with the international community.

Long demonstrates an appreciation of Francis' renewed vision for the church, one that includes an approach to the key issues of social policy, challenges aimed at alleviating global inequality and climate change. We discover from Long that Francis' reflective praxis is innovate in two ways, the first essentially political and the second deeply spiritual, both elements in Francis are mutually reinforcing. In highlighting the faith-political synthesis of Francis, Long allows us to understand something of the Pope's call for a cultural renewal of the fundamental precepts that ground our economic life. Francis prefers to focus upon a praxis of engagement which emphasises a pastoral and deeply spiritual connection with all people, especially those who are marginalised.

Long argues that there can be no doubt that Francis presents a kerygmatic challenge and call for metanoia to the economic community. Employing a humorous sporting analogy Long depicts Francis to be in a cricket game against a World Economic XI. In *Evangelli Gaudium*, Francis bowled fast and short; having warmed up sufficiently in *Laudato Si*, Francis finds line and length and is highly critical of contemporary economic institutions. The Pope's critique of economic forces and their detrimental effects on the poor and marginalised is strident and confronting. He understands the current neo-liberal economic mantra as a culture that kills. The constant search for prosperity erodes us from within spiritually as we succumb to the delusive allure of personal consumption. Long concludes that Francis is presenting the world with a positive message grounded in a Christian spirituality of economic asceticism, one that should be adopted for the sake of the common good. Further, Francis' prophetic voice is neither a morose nor dour asceticism; but rather a joyous undertaking that finds liberation through the enlargement of the common good in the praise of God's gift of creation.

In Chapter, Eight **Frank Brennan** discerns the place for the prophetic voice and pragmatic co-operation of the churches in the great moral questions of the age. He insists that whoever would lead someone to faith needs the ability to speak well and reason properly without violence and threats. A good speaker knows their audience and speaks to their predispositions and historical consciousness. The prophetic voice according to Brennan has more chance of being heard when it resonates not with jingoistic nationalism, but when it accords with the audience's sense of their abiding values and salvation history, marked out on their own land and their time.

Offering his own prophetic voice to speak for the rights of refugees, Brennan praises Australian church leaders for publishing fine and lofty statements about rights of asylum seekers, but asks where is the church agency with the mandate to follow up on the fine church statements, calling our elected leaders to account. Religious leaders in the public square are charged to emulate Pope Francis, raising a prophetic voice, appealing to the noble aspirations of the public. Equally important, people of faith who hold public office are also called to be a public voice of reason, speaking out for those suffering and championing the pursuit of truth in an age increasingly labelled as *post-truth*.

Brennan invites religious leaders to awaken in our political leaders and the public that still, small voice of conscience. Indeed, the prophetic message or the still, small voice of conscience is best amplified in Australia not by religious leaders, but according to Brennan, by poets, novelists and folk singers. With reference to the appalling treatment of refugees and migrants by the Australian government, the acclaimed Australian novelist Tim Winton observed, 'I may be no expert..., but I know when something is wrong. And what my country is doing is wrong'.

Explaining how his appreciation of *Laudato Si* was enhanced by Rowan Williams, Brennan illustrates the importance of ecumenical dialogue, a primary principle of APTO. Indeed, ecumenical dialogue and praxis is an essential precondition for any meaningful engagement by church leaders in the public square. Drawing upon his experience as Chair of the Commission to examine the potential of an Australian Bill of Rights, Brennan concludes, that if the churches can't agree on a moral basis for arguments about inequality, climate change, same sex marriage or euthanasia, we cannot expect our politicians to take distinctive religious argument as much more than quaint observations. Brennan insists, 'without trust between those whose conscience differ we will not incarnate the mystery of the Godhead'.

Finally, and in appropriating the inspirational thought of Brennan, we can say that this book seeks to speak with freedom and integrity and to offer a prophetic voice in what sometimes feels like a wilderness of contemporary political discourse. There are risks involved with such effort, of polarisation and disparagement, of being misheard or misrepresented. And yet, pace Brennan, grounded in our social reality, alert to the claims of those who are marginalised and suffering ongoing injustice, the authors in this book equally inspired by their still, small voice of conscience, seek to engage theology in the public square, to 'give reason to the hope that is within them' (1 Peter 3:15).

Chapter One

Fundamentalisms and the Emergence of the Post-Secular Age[1]

Anthony Maher

Introduction: The Secular Age

Sounding like an epitaph, whilst attracting little public lament, our time is frequently characterised as the Secular Age. Charles Taylor in his seminal tome The Secular Age begins to define secularity as the separation of religion from the state. He writes,

> ... the political organisation of all pre-modern societies was in some way connected to, based on, guaranteed by some faith in, or adherence to God, or some notion of ultimate reality, the modern Western state is free from this connection.[2]

Drawing upon the implications of Taylor's insight, this chapter will explore the apparent rise of fundamentalisms in the so-called Secular Age, an epoch paradoxically characterised by its rejection 'of notions of ultimate reality'. In a Western context this rejection or paradigmatic shift is arguably responsible for a deepening sense of loss around notions of God, truth, and reason for *being*. A further layer of cultural complexity derives from the experience of globalisation and multiculturalism, which further tests individual and group notions of identity and belonging. A consequence of the above two realities sees a post-modern cultural vacuum developing, characterised in part by identity confusion. Into this deepening void strides movements or subcultures which can be understood as fundamentalist in their worldview. Such movements project simplistic answers, offering a supposed

---

[1] The chapter is inspired by the seminal work of the cultural anthropologist Rev Dr Gerald A. Arbuckle SM
[2] Charles Taylor, *The Secular Age*, (Cambridge, Massachusetts: Harvard University Press, 2007), 1.

fundamentalist panacea to placate cultural anxiety around complex questions of identity and notions of ultimate reality. Such cultural movements, as we will see in proceeding chapters, lead some scholars to describe our time as post-secular.

Gerald A. Arbuckle shows that historically the term *fundamentalism* originated from attempts to protect notions of Christian orthodoxy from the perceived threat of liberalism.[3] During the course of the twentieth century and the ascendency of secular thinking, the term fundamentalism morphed into a pejorative denotation to describe a radicalised belief system characterised by a closed meta-narrative not only applicable to religions, but also to extreme forms of nationalism and other formulae of ideological thinking, such as excessive free-market economics or neo-liberalism. This latter mentality became associated with hegemonic far-right groups such as the ('Invisible hands'), *Americans for Prosperity Foundation* and the closely allied *Tea Party* movement.[4]

This chapter will critique, from the perspective of an anti-foundationalist epistemology, three prevalent examples of closed-truth fundamentalist notions of 'ultimate reality': (i) religious fundamentalism, (ii) proselytising atheism, and (iii) uncompromising neo-liberalism. The chapter will move on to test the above three virulent responses to the question of post-modern insecurity before concluding with a prolegomenon to a fourth evolving pathway. The fourth pathway under discussion seeks to be a relevant response to post-modern insecurity and involves a diachronic and synchronic *modus operandi*. A way of being cognisant of a chastened Christianity, a faith modelled upon the humble servant of Isaiah, a liberated and 'refounding' Christianity situated at the crossroads of post modernity.

The classic Marxist critique with regard to class division can be of assistance in shedding some light on the causes of the contemporary manifestation of fundamentalisms and the juxtaposed authentic

---

[3] For a detailed discussion, history and definition of the term *fundamentalism* see Gerald A. Arbuckle, *Fundamentalism at Home and Abroad: Analysis and Pastoral Response.* (Collegeville, Minnesota: Liturgical Press, 2017), 1-29.

[4] 'The Billionaires Bankrolling the Tea Party', Frank Rich, *The New York Times,* August 28, 2010, Accessed 26/5/17. http://www.nytimes.com/2010/08/29/opinion/29rich.html.Accessed 20 July 2016.

pursuit of human liberation.⁵ Arguably the three forms of oppressive fundamentalism under discussion here are a consequence of economic class division, perpetrated primarily by elites who strive to "colonise" culture, pace Feuerbach, to form culture in their own image. Such hegemonic behaviour fosters division though control of: information, research, media, technology, medicine, money, food, clean air, water, armaments and, perhaps most discriminatory of all, education. In controlling education, including the dispossession of education to marginalised peoples, hegemonic powers adopt Orwellian doublespeak of using language to mislead or conceal information, to engineer cultural narratives, and form a Nietzschean consciousness devoid of human dignity.

In sum, the world is once again experiencing an 'interregnum', to draw upon Italian political theorist Antonio Gramsci and his vivid description of a world in crisis. 'The crisis consists precisely in the fact that the old is dying and the new cannot be born; in this interregnum a great variety of morbid symptoms appear.'⁶ Interregnums are dangerous and doubly morbid if unaccompanied by a readiness to think anew about changed power structures. From Gramsci's perspective, such a changed power structure would by definition acknowledge that there can be no freedom for one, unless there is emancipation for all. Three contemporary closed-truth morbid symptoms (fundamentalisms) are critiqued below, along with a fourth Christian open-truth midwifery resolution to these signs of our times, one engaged in refounding Christianity from the ashes of colonialism, the Holocaust and two twentieth century world wars.

The fourth pathway advocates for a changed power structure, one built upon economic, political, social and religious emancipation of the oppressed. To escape charges of idealism, the fourth pathway requires a contemporary theological anthropology, including a refounding of the doctrine of Original Sin. Such endeavour is also a work of emancipation, waiting for the old theology to die, so that the new liberated theology may be born.

---

⁵ See the critique of Neo-liberalism below as a closed truth meta-narrative and the prophetic work of South American liberation theologians such as Gustavo Gutierrez, Ignacio Ellacuría, Jon Sobrino, Juan Luis Segundo Leonardo Boff *et al.*

⁶ Antonio Gramsci, cited in Davidson's, *Antonio Gramsci: Towards an Intellectual Biography*, (London: Merlin Press, [1977]) 77.

Finally, by way of introduction, a brief caveat. Attempts at defining the secular age, or the possible emergence of a post-secular epoch are fraught with risk. Such endeavour, portraying or critiquing one's own time or culture, is not dissimilar to an intoxicated artist attempting a self-portrait in poor light. We must acknowledge that we are producing an inexact picture, and must therefore remain mindful of the hermeneutics of suspicion. Hence, all attempts to understand our own reality are communicated and subsequently received through a contextual cultural landscape. Nevertheless, there is value in an impressionist portrait. Further complexity unfolds for our endeavour as we add into our contemporary cultural matrix: the rise of a radical atheism, post-modern identity confusion and the subsequent escalation of home-grown fundamentalisms, religious and political. The chapter will highlight evidence that suggests our time is experiencing an emergence of 'morbid symptoms' in the form of numerous fundamentalist confessions. Such morbid movements practise aggressive proselytisation and globalisation, while other manifestations advocate for isolationism and a rejection of multiculturalism. In unison and perhaps most notable, such fundamentalist schools of 'morbid thought' are characterised by a closed-truth meta-narrative.

A Closed Meta-Narrative (I): Religion as a Form of Contemporary Fundamentalism

The prophet of religious fundamentalism is akin to the Siren of Greek methodology, a dangerous Siren who with enchanting music and words lures the "lost mariner" to shipwreck on the rocky coast of life. Not too dissimilar to the unreasonable mantra of the orthodox Marxist, adherents of a closed truth religious meta-narrative are recognised by their inability to countenance an alternative point of view. Masked in an absolutist denial that other religious truth claims may have validity, similar to the absolutist *persona* worn by the orthodox Marxist, a closed truth religious meta-narrative (Cathedral / Mosque) is open to micro and macro forms of totalitarianism. A closed-religious meta-narrative is built upon a foundationalist epistemology and in all things asserts a deductive certainty. Religious prophets seek to lure the philosophically perplexed (the emotionally vulnerable) into an illusory safe harbour, enticed by seductive, often sexual, melodious promises of eschatological bliss. They promise all-consuming meta-narratives of salvation from the imagined storm of post-modern cultural pluralism, *pace*, relativist dictatorships of decadence.

The French post-modern philosopher Jean-Francois Lyotard challenged the legitimacy of these all-consuming meta-narratives, deductive ideas that since the Enlightenment have "explained" reality.[7] Lyotard argued (1979) that modernity had become philosophically disillusioned with closed-truth grandiose claims of meta-narratives. Four decades on and the overwhelming cultural (social, economic and political) presence of pluralist narrower *petits récits* ("little narratives"), is manifest and undeniable. Such "little narrative" discourse empowers the marginalised to be heard and history to be rewritten to include the voice of the voiceless. Lyotard developed Wittgenstein's 'language games' to create a linguistic framework of meaning in which *petits récits* can be understood as narratives that contain their own internal integrity. The postmodern political challenge is to respect and accommodate difference, while at the same time, building consensus around universal ethical norms of justice.

Lyotard understood closed meta-narratives as self-serving sources of power (fascism, communism, neo-liberalism, religious fundamentalism), divisive by intent, projecting intolerance of difference, and ultimately socially destructive. Postmodern anti-foundationalist epistemologies remain juxtaposed to universalising philosophies or political totalitarian ideologies. Simply, Lyotard maintains that closed-truth meta-narratives are no longer adequate to explain our post-modern reality. We are becoming 'alert to difference', so indeed it seems reasonable to posit that the demise of closed-truth meta-narratives and the growing awareness of diversity is a hope filled promise for the future of the planet and humanity. The abundance and potential of *petits récits* ("little narratives"), is easily illustrated in the abundant diversity (and delight) of postmodern cuisine.

---

[7] See for example the seminal works by Jean-Francois Lyotard, *La Condition Postmoderne: Rapport sur le Savoir*, (Editions de Minuit, 1979), *and The Differend: Phrases in Dispute* (Les Editions de Minuit,1983).

Humanity has sought religious meaning for existence down through millennia. Most cultures found solace through a closed-truth meta-narrative of faith in a God(s). Faith in a transcendent being or heavenly reality gave "closed" meaning to all historical human societies. A philosophical question which arises in our time, perhaps unique to our time, is how societies might, where God is no longer the answer, seek an alternative point of reference for *being*. Thus Lyotard became highly critical of the faith religious people placed in the totality of unquestioned belief. His sceptical critique of closed meta-narratives is a position increasingly adopted by cultures that are fortunate to experience widely available university education. Increasingly, western societies are rejecting closed religious meta-narratives, with their subsequent all-encompassing world view, one that resolutely refuses to dialogue with alternative or complementary understandings of reality.

The United State is unlike any other Western nation in the sense that a particular form of religious allegiance is regularly manifest. Republicans habitually seek to "out-pray" the Democrats. In essence, both seek to capture the all-important religious vote. On the global stage, religion is frequently presented as a cause of war. It is most often presented as the motivation for the current wave of Islamic terrorism that is devastating the Middle East and causing terror and displacement, from Abuja to Mogadishu, from London, Paris, Manchester, Madrid and Moscow to Bangkok, Bali, Berlin and New York. The list of nation cities plagued by terrorism continues to grow.

Despite the best efforts of secularists and radical atheists, forms of religion are experiencing resurgence in contemporary consciousness, particularly amongst marginalised peoples and alienated youth. Major world religions, perhaps, in part, as a misguided attempt to combat a post-modern induced identity crisis, appear to be increasingly fundamentalist in their critique of 'western' reality. Religions are seeking to proselytise youth directly from outside the traditional family micro context. They offer philosophical certainty (truth) in exchange for freedom of conscience and intellectual, evidential enquiry. Such religious groups present a powerful and alluring counter-cultural critique to idealistic or socially marginalised youth, offering certainty and belonging in a climate characterised by uncertainty and pluralism.

On the cultural plain of post-modernity, it is not too difficult to fathom why there is little public discussion with regard to the decline of institutional Christianity. Equally absent is any discussion with regard to what may be lost to wider society, as a consequence of the continuing decline of religious belief. For many, religion is a "tough-gig"; in a Christian context church, adherence can be "heavy-going". Our secular culture also appears to be experiencing a growing apathy or indifference towards challenging questions of existence and transcendence. In a Western context, such cultural drift away from Christianity, indicative of modern relativist living, is exacerbated by our post-modern existentialist resolve, an inward-looking preoccupation with the self rather than community or even family. A reality characterised by a growing resistance to all external forms of religion and governmental (political) institutions of authority – opposing all those who would 'seek power over us'. Reminiscent of Mel Gibson's caricature of William Wallace *(Braveheart)*, we all in unison cry: "freedom". A consequence of this 'cry freedom' is evident in the Arab Spring, Brexit and Donald Trump.

On the spiritual plane, a further possible response to the 'cry freedom' might be that post-moderns desire freedom from our materialistic self. Perhaps we are motivated by the unarticulated recognition that we continue to drift ever further away from knowledge of the transcendent. One response to this cultural shift away from God draws an increasing number of people to religious fundamentalist 'schools of thought' that offer certainty, a God rationalised by humanity, God neatly framed within a closed quasi-philosophical meta-narrative. The God Feuerbach clearly foresaw, made in humanities own image. Frantically, as Feuerbach rightly suggested, we seek to create God in our own image; today, fundamentalist thinking strives to give meaning to our reality as a belief system closed to any alterative world view.

Religious fundamentalism is a form of organised anger. In a religious context, it materialises as a social movement in 'reaction to secularism, neo-liberalism and globalisation. It often intimidates or coerces people unduly to achieve its ends.'[8] No religion is immune from this growing global phenomenon, Judaism has seen the return of

---

[8] Gerald A. Arbuckle, *Violence, Society, and the Church: A Cultural Approach* (Collegeville, MN: Liturgical Press, 2004), 213.

the Orwellian "modesty police," an ultra-orthodox movement known as the *Haredi*, who send men to patrol public transport in order to segregate men from women and ensure that women sit at the back and refrain from "inappropriate" dress. Following the 9/11 massacre in New York, the rise of fundamental Islam among the most vulnerable and dispossessed is well documented. Hindu extremists have also been responsible for the most terrifying outrages, and the so-called Christian 'crusade' led by George W. Bush launched 'shock and awe' upon the long-suffering people of Iraq and Afghanistan. Syria and Iraq have experienced the rise of *Daesh* and a continuing civil war that has left thousands dead and millions displaced.

In the post Brexit world of Northern Ireland, religious sectarianism refuses to dissipate, whilst recent decades witnessed "Catholic bombs" exploding and Protestants who sought bloody revenge. On the Indian sub-continent, Hindus and Muslims continue to exclude or oppose each other at any given opportunity. Chechen Islamists, in the hope of martyrdom and heavenly rewards engaged in the mass murder of Beslan school children. In the Middle East, the banner of religious fundamentalism continues to incite the young to a clarion call to violence and hatred resulting in countless deaths of innocent people. Further examples include: *Sunni* fighting *Shi'ite* in Iraq; *Hamas* is combating *Fatah* in Palestine; *Jihadist* seeking to slaughter Jews on buses in the market place of Jerusalem; Israel retaliating with occupation, tanks, and ballistic missiles. Syrian backed *Hezbollah* raining terror on Christians in Lebanon and Jews in Israel; the Islamic Republic of Iran rushing into the nuclear arms race in opposition to Israel and the USA; Indonesian Islamists killing tourists; university educated British Muslims murdering their own citizens; the Taliban prophesying that religious terror will return to Afghanistan and the elusive *Al Qaeda*, harnessing brainwashed children to commit mass murder wherever possible, to bring about a Western (Christian) Armageddon, and the establishment of Sharia law in an Islamic state. It seems Blaise Pascal (1623-1662) was right, 'we never do evil so fully and cheerfully as when we do it out of religious conviction.'[9]

---

[9] *Educating Hearts*, 'religious fundamentalism', Anthony Maher and Bob Hanley, (Strathfield: St Paul's Publications, 2013), 28-30.

Throughout human history, religion is recorded as the rallying cry to inspire by what we hold most dear, the flag to hoist stirring humanity to action: 'Cry for God, Harry, England and St George' had little to do with belief in the Gospel of Jesus Christ and had everything to do with conquest, greed and the desire for power. Deeds of terror from a faith perspective are self-proclaiming acts of excommunication in both Islam and Christianity. The perpetrators in the act of terror place themselves outside the faith tradition.[10] Religion has ever thus been exploited by those with a personal, political, nationalistic or ideological agenda. It is not God's agenda.

Indeed, religious fundamentalism unchallenged inspires acts of terrorism. A critique of terrorism requires an understanding of the causes of terror along with a forthright condemnation of those who seek to terrorise. Understandably the growth of religious fundamentalism is causing concern and increasing fear and division within society. There are many examples of ground swell movements towards fundamentalism. The formative work of cultural anthropologist Gerald A. Arbuckle has sought to track this growing phenomenon over many decades. In earlier work, he considered fundamentalism to be 'a historically recurring tendency within Judeo-Christian-Muslim religious traditions, [which] occurs as an authoritarian reaction to the fears of chaos evoked by postmodernism and globalisation.'[11] Arbuckle understands fundamentalists to be,

> ...people who are outraged when they see the world around them abandoning the religious values they hold dear. They are fighting back in the cause of what they consider truth. They are reacting to threats to their identity in militant ways, whether in the use of words and ideas or ballots or, in extreme cases, bullets and bombs. The responses to these threats are simplistic and those who question them are intolerantly branded as enemies of the truth.[12]

---

[10] Muhammed Sadar ud Dean Sahu Khan, *Is takfir allowed in Islam? Excommunication of a Muslim from the religion of Islam*, (Canberra, CSU, 2015).

[11] Gerald A. Arbuckle, *Violence, Society, and the Church: A Cultural Approach* (Collegeville, MN: Liturgical Press, 2004), 195. See also Gerald A. Arbuckle, *Fundamentalism at Home and Abroad: Analysis and Pastoral Responses* (Collegeville, MN: Liturgical Press, 2017), 1.

[12] Gerald A. Arbuckle, *Fundamentalism at Home and Abroad: Analysis and Pastoral Responses* (Collegeville, MN: Liturgical Press, 2017), 1.

A public religion running on empty acquiesces with secular thinking that tolerates God, but would confine God to the heavens, in a sort of a back to the future return to a medieval cosmological world view. Such belief understands God never earthed, a distant God to be feared, even a God of the fundamentalist. The secular narrative holds that God may not be dead, but that he no longer directs the ebb and flow of life down here on earth. With Thomas Hardy, it is tempting to muse that God lives on, but has fled the heaven in which humanity sought to imprison him. In the poet's mind, God has forgotten the human race, 'The Earth? Nay: I have no remembrance of such place: Such world I fashioned not… Haply it died of doing as it durst?'[13]

Taylor draws on the prophetic thought of the former Jesuit George Tyrrell to describe how Western culture sought to produce a tamed version of Christianity, a God custom-made to suit our demands. Such a view contrived to find,

> A moralist in a visionary; a professor in a prophet; the nineteenth century in the first; the natural in the supernatural. Christ was the ideal man; the kingdom of heaven, the ideal humanity. As the rationalistic presupposition had strained out, as spurious, the miraculous elements in the Gospels, so the moralistic presupposition strained out everything but modern morality. That alone was the substance, the essence of Christianity.[14]

Scholars such as Yves Congar and Charles Taylor consider the shift to public secularity, brought about perhaps by religion running on empty, has played a significant role in creating what we call the Secular Age. Such an age is understood as the decline of belief and practice, along with faith in God being perceived as one possibility amongst many others. In 1934, the *ressourcement* theologian Congar predicted such an eventuality when he foresaw that,

---

[13] 'God Forgotten', *Selected Poems of Thomas Hardy*, (1940), 113-114.
[14] See George Tyrrell, *Christianity at the Crossroads*, (London: Longmans, Green and Co, 2nd Impression, 1910), 42. Quoted in Charles Taylor, *The Secular Age*, 292, 806 and Alister McGrath, *The Twilight of Atheism*, (2004), 140. See also Anthony Maher, *The Forgotten Jesuit of Catholic Modernism*, (Augsburg Fortress Press, 2018).

As long as we have not done the theology of all the great human realities that must be won back for Christ, we will not have done the first thing that is to be done... An enormous task of information, investigation, contacts and right-minded, ardent, living reflection lies before us. We must prepare, on the austere, laborious level of theological science, to reconquer the modern world. But the first condition for doing theology is believing in it.[15]

In a secular context, humanity seeks to come of age and proclaim humanity. Increasingly, secular institutions, governments, universities and commercial enterprises, produce mission statements, whilst asserting their secular autonomy from the hegemonic synthesis of crown and altar. In so doing, contemporary institutions challenge an historical reality which arguably dominated the geo-political world for millennia.

In most respects the secular age is indifferent to religion, so long as people of faith do not seek to dominate legal and political decision-making processes. Western nations such as the USA have devised important laws to ensure religions "give to Caesar what belongs to Caesar". In other words, secular culture tolerates moderate religious adherence but not political interference. The challenge still remains, from a Christian perspective of orthopraxis (right-living), that faith is lived in the real world rather than in deductive or abstract thought. Such belief systems as Christianity, require public and political advocacy for social justice, particularly for the oppressed and the marginalised within society.

(ii) Radical Atheism as a Form of Contemporary Fundamentalism

A possible consequence or reaction to the growing awareness of the link between religion and fundamentalism is the resurgence in the public space of non-religious stake holders in the form of high profile evangelical atheists. Such champions of intolerance regularly ridicule those who hold faith in God and insist on denouncing the religious

---

[15] Yves *Congar, 'Déficit de la théologie'*, *Explorations in Practical Theology: Bridging the Divide Between Faith, Theology and Life*, (Editor) Anthony Maher, (Adelaide: ATF Press 2015), 38.

voice on numerous concerns ranging from the environment, education to philosophy and public ethics.[16] Such 'celebrities' encouraged by a too compliant sensationalist media, dominate public discourse on religion, reminiscent of Nietzsche's madman with the lamp, and new atheism in the form of Singer, Dawkins, Krauss *et-al* replacing the earlier anti-theologians, Feuerbach, Nietzsche, and Freud. Contemporary evangelical atheists espouse a closed meta-narrative of truth, which in many respects belongs to another age. Such closed narrative defines 'our' story as 'the' story, and remains opposed to any other open truth-seeking narrative.

Taylor emphasised that our 'political society is seen as that of believers and non-believers alike' and that '…our public spaces have been emptied of God'. Such a position is similar in context to what Yves Congar prophetically signalled in the 1930s as the potential of our culture to become disincarnate. In considering the birth of the post-God secular epoch, one is drawn further back to the nineteenth century and to Nietzsche's prophetic parable of the madman who lit a lantern in the bright morning hours, rampaging into the market place seeking the elusive God.

The madman jumped into their midst and pierced them with his eyes. 'Whither is God?' he cried; 'I will tell you. We have killed him - you and I. All of us are his murderers'.

The madman continues: now that we have killed God, removed him from the public space, 'how will we comfort ourselves?' 'What was holiest and mightiest of all that the world has yet owned has bled to death under our knives: who will wipe this blood off us?'

Nietzsche is lamenting the death of Christ on the cross, 'put to death by our knives'. The madman asks, 'how did we do this?' How did we put God to death? In the context of the secular age, one might reasonably conclude it was the barbarism of the twentieth century – 'that did for Him!' Perhaps allowing insight into Nietzsche's own 'will to power', the madman smashed his lantern on the ground and yelled to the crowd, 'I have come too early, my time is not yet.' From the perspective of radical atheism, perhaps the madman's time is now?

---

[16] For example, see Richard Dawkins, *God Delusion* (London: Transworld Publishers Ltd. 2006), selling over three million copies and translated into thirty-five languages.

Certainly the new atheist movements of our time are becoming ever more vocal. Their vitriolic critique of religious faith resonates strongly with xenophobic proliferating forces of fear and division. Contemporary atheism has become ever more evangelical, morphing into an ideological worldview intent on proselytising, whilst xenophobic fear of the other (refugee, Muslim, stranger) joins with the atheistic call to silence the religious voice. Such atheistic attempts that seek to marginalise religion find support from the doyens of a western liberal media who see religion as opposing the autonomy of individualism and moral relativism.

New atheism seeks to proselytise. Adherents boldly proclaim in the public market place of ideas, not so much that God is dead, for that would imply original existence, but rather that the 'idea' of God is dead. Martin Amis cleverly articulated the atheist position that seeks to dominate Western culture: Europe has outgrown religion, Amis argued. 'Simply outgrown it... we've waited it out and it is gone'. *Pace* the Global Financial Crash and the Western neo-liberal commodification of relationships, indeed our culture appears increasingly devoid of a credible ethical compass, allowing Amis' popular cultural caricature to enjoy a certain critical resonance.

Undeniably, and in a myriad of ways through millennia, humanity has sought faith in God to satisfy a deep human need, a quest for meaning that secures belonging, only to be dissatisfied by a competing reality. Such cultural security, if ever obtained, was most certainly shaken to the core by the dreadfulness of two world wars and the holocaust. Indeed, C.S. Lewis's wartime BBC radio broadcasts, later published as the classic *Mere Christianity*, sought to provide a Christian apologetic to the pain and suffering induced by the two wars and to answer the question that is human suffering.[17] As the decades advance and the two world wars fade from living memory, almost with each passing year we see the decline of the United Nations and the rise of nationalistic closed meta-narratives.

The secular narrative appreciates that Anthropocene humanity has fulfilled the potential of the Enlightenment, breaking free from the shackles of superstition and religion. Such narrative understands

---

[17] *C S Lewis A Life*, Alister McGrath, (London: Hodder & Stoughton, 2013), 191-213.

that humankind has out-grown a medieval or scholastic world-view, one that sought to placate human reason by rationalising a "God of the Gaps" hypothesis. Today, secular thinking generally tolerates religious adherence whilst insisting that religious sentiment plays little more than a ceremonial role within Western culture. Indeed, little soul searching accompanies the separation of God from the idea of God. Western culture, by a gradual process of osmosis, and not revolution, but equally epoch defining, has become adept at separating notions of "God" from organised religion.

Interestingly, contemporary Western culture seems to have little difficulty making the distinction between belief in some form of postmodern spirituality and institutional religion. Sociological evidence suggests, in an Australian context for example, that most Catholics reject religious adherence although seemingly maintain a spiritual belief system of some description. The increasing reality of people believing and not belonging leads Habermas to ask poignantly, 'can we do believing without belonging or whether the gradual attrition of de-institutionalisation will result, eventually, in public religion running on empty.'

In his *Secular Age*, Taylor moves on to consider that an age or society would be secular or not, 'in virtue of the conditions of experience of and search for the spiritual'. One needs to look closely at the history of the past century to uncover experiences of the spiritual, certainly such insight is not gleamed from the news we read on our PC or iPhone.[18] Whilst we are perhaps experiencing the growth of public religious consciousness, it seems uncertain - from a theological perspective - that it is anything more than a political-ideological world view. Most likely, within a secular context, we are experiencing the development of global secularism and the consequential micro and macro clash of cultures. Arguably, the reasoned connection between faith in the transcendent God and the prevailing tide of quasi-religious fundamentalism is at best tenuous.

---

[18] Taylor, *The Secular Age*, 3.

(iii) Neo-liberalism as a form of Contemporary Fundamentalism

Fundamentalist thinking is not restricted to religion. Unlike colonialists dividing continents, today it is difficult to draw a line to separate the borders between what constitutes religious or political fundamentalism. Political discourse throughout the Twentieth Century testifies to radical movements of ideological polarisation, including the rise of totalitarianism in Russia and China, along with the attempted fascist takeover of Western Europe (Hitler, Mussolini, Franco). Such closed meta-narrative voices in Europe have thankfully diminished but they have not gone away.

In the Western context, much public discourse is generated by those who support the neoliberal agenda, including the dominance of so-called "free" market economics. Neo-liberalism is an economic-political form of fundamentalism, which posits the rights of the individual over and above the common good, a movement personified by Trumpism, one that largely precipitated the global financial crash, the rise of the Tea Party in the US and arguably created a vacuum of reasonableness filled by self-serving populism. Truth was jettisoned for "truthful hyperbole", which allowed Donald Trump to propel himself into the White House. Once respected news media outlets now produce "False News" for our so-called "post-Truth Age". Western culture will pay a high price for encouraging news to become 24 hour entertainment. In so doing, journalism gave way to Hollywood hyperbole, where a sensational or salacious story pays more than reporting the facts or researching for hard evidence.

In the political arena also, communication is not always transparent. Much of contemporary political discourse is pejoratively employed to dehumanise. Increasingly, political language is not interested in conveying truth, words become false to the facts, and performance takes priority over the descriptive with socially calamitous consequences. Polarising division within society is further exacerbated by the rise of so-called religious fundamentalism, plundering neo-liberalism and the moral failure of western capitalism to share the fruits of globalisation. Concurrently, western democracies are experiencing arguably, the greatest ever decline in public confidence, whilst our politicians are perceived to be out of touch with the majority of 'real' people. Politicians appear reliant upon polls and rhetorical spin to deceive in order to preserve their own existing positions of power and privilege.

Experts on climate change or economics who dare to offer an opposing view to the closed meta-narrative of neo-liberalism are publicly vilified by politicians and their media associates. One of the most unforgettable examples of performance over descriptive came from the 2016 Brexit debate when Michael Gove, the UK Minister of Education, challenged economists who forecast that the UK economy would be damaged by Brexit. Gove proclaimed in the Murdoch media, 'Britain has had enough of experts'. Apparently Britain has had enough of facts, knowledge, evidence, education, truth!

Such manufactured falsehoods are increasingly common and foster division witnessed notably in the electoral success of Donald Trump in the USA, Rodrigo Duterte in the Philippines and Pauline Hanson in Australia, not forgetting a growing number of nationalistic politicians across Europe who fraternise the disenfranchised – real and imagined. Arguably, we are also experiencing in a western secular context the continued growth of fringe political parties who openly peddle a closed-truth meta-narrative of social, economic and political division. Neo-liberalism represents an agenda of division - one that intentionally commodifies relationships and nullifies strategies to enhance the common good through social-economic interrelationships.

The not unconnected political equivalent to religious apathy outlined above sees the rise of fringe political parties and individuals. Examples are not limited to Pauline Hanson's *One Nation* in Australia, and include Nigel Farage's *Ukip* in Britain, as well as numerous right wing movements across Europe, such as Marine Le Pen's *National Front* in France and Heinz-Christian Strache's *Freedom Party of Austria*. As nations look ever more inward and pursue protectionist policies, there can be little surprise that the United Nations is becoming increasingly irrelevant on the world stage. Boutros-Ghali, Kofi Annan, Ban Ki-Moon all former UN Secretaries-General were household names. I wonder how well known is the current Secretary-General?

While it seems to be the case that mainstream religious institutions in the West are in decline, it is also the case that political institutions or parties are in disarray. Decreasing affiliation to conventional political movements replicates the steady decline in religious adherence. The cumulative absence of moderate religious voices within our culture creates a vacuum. If the religious vacuum is filled with fundamentalist possibilities on one pole, the other culturally extreme pole trends towards an emerging ethical nihilism, fed by the growth of materialism and relativism. From a theological perspective, a crucial question arises, how might we reclaim the moderate middle ground currently occupied by religious apathy? Equally challenging is the need on the part of theologians to articulate a cogent clarion call to the "moral majority", that we might awake from religious slumbers and possibly become defenders of minority groups, such as dispossessed peoples, and awake our culture to champion the common good.

As mentioned earlier, it is important to acknowledge the insights that may be gleaned from the application of classical Marxist analysis to our contemporary socio-economic context and the consequential rise of modern formulations of fundamentalism. Arguably, the three forms of fundamentalism under discussion in this chapter are a consequence of economic class division. Any practical response that seeks to moderate the consequences of fundamentalism must include a commitment to economic justice for all humanity. There will not be peace for one person until there is justice for all. Such *Perestroika* and *Glasnost* wisdom concerning economics is echoed in the thought of Nobel peace prize recipient Mikhail Gorbachev (1990), and in the seminal teaching of Pope Paul VI (1967). For example, Gorbachev considered Jesus to be the first socialist, the first to seek a better life for humanity,

Neo-liberalism profits from increasing the economic divide, together with the subsequent and increasing powerlessness of labour. To this end, hegemonic consortia (self-serving multinationals, huge investment banks and media outlets) control wealth, health and education. Sadly and again increasingly through the neo-liberal strategy of outsourcing government responsibilities to private sector conglomerates, (health, aged-care, social welfare, prisons, education, water, electricity, technology, transport) it is becoming ever more difficult to untangle the role of government from privately owned multinationals.

Neo-liberal inspired multinationals exist simply to acquire profit. They increasingly present as unfeeling automata, operating like a machine, without evidence of human conscience. Mega-businesses devour competition and natural resources, as robots designed for a particular task regardless of social consequence. Multinationals are programmed to respond to economic stimuli, they are relatively self-operating. Multinationals follow a predetermined sequence of operations in order to respond to market fluctuations to maximise investment returns. Ever responding to market fluctuations, most conglomerates give the illusion to the casual investor - like gongs or clanging cymbals in mechanical clocks - that they are operating to an ethical code of conduct or freely engaging in philanthropy. In essence, such acts of charity remain prone to mechanistic market stimuli; often designed to appear aesthetically pleasing, their purpose is calculated to increase profit. Until multinationals adjust their percentage income, proportionate to size of profit, and engage in a just redistribution of wealth based upon human dignity and social need, such random acts of charity will ever remain, as St Paul suggests, suspect with regard to intention.

> If I speak in the tongues of men or of angels, but do not have love, I am only a resounding gong or a clanging cymbal. If I have the gift of prophecy and can fathom all mysteries and all knowledge, and if I have a faith that can move mountains, but do not have love, I am nothing. If I give all I possess to the poor and give over my body to hardship that I may boast, but do not have love, I gain nothing.[19]

Pope Paul VI insisted that 'economic development is the new name for peace.' Recognising a possible drift towards totalitarian ideologies, as a consequence of economic injustice, Paul VI counselled,

---

[19] 1 Corinthians 13:1.

> In such troubled times some people are strongly tempted by the alluring but deceitful promises of would-be saviours. Who does not see the concomitant dangers: public upheavals, civil insurrection, the drift toward totalitarian ideologies?[20]

The Pope insisted that 'unbridled liberalism paves the way for a particular type of tyranny... for it results in the international imperialism of money. Such improper manipulations of economic forces can never be condemned enough; let it be said once again that economics is supposed to be in the service of man.'[21]

> The hungry nations of the world cry out to the peoples blessed with abundance. And the Church, cut to the quick by this cry, asks each and every man to hear his brother's plea and answer it lovingly. Then there are the flagrant inequalities not merely in the enjoyment of possessions, but even more in the exercise of power. In certain regions a privileged minority enjoys the refinements of life, while the rest of the inhabitants, impoverished and disunited, are deprived of almost all possibility of acting on their own initiative and responsibility, and often subsist in living and working conditions unworthy of the human person.[22]

Paul VI makes the nuanced distinction between the common benefits of industrialisation itself and the evils that derive from the pernicious economic concepts (neoliberalism) that grew up alongside industrial development. The means of production in the mind of Paul VI has but one aim: to serve human nature. The ultimate purpose of economic growth is to serve the common good. Neoliberalism speaks the language of the dollar. Reality is viewed through the prism of the dollar. Mental health is an issue of dollars lost to the economy; the Great Barrier Reef is worth, according to Deloitte Access Economics, $56 billion. Reality has become subservient to the dollar. When we speak of economic development we should mean social progress for all humanity. Neo-liberalism considers social progress as an impediment to economic hegemonic prosperity, (example, Trump's

---

[20] *Populorum Progressio*, Encyclical of Pope Paul VI 'On The Development Of Peoples', 26 March 1967, 11.
[21] *Populorum Progressio*, 26.
[22] *Populorum Progressio*, 3.

repeal of Obama's health reforms - a safety net for the most vulnerable in society). In this sense, neoliberalism dehumanises and is perhaps a far more insidious threat to humanity than religious fundamentalism.

Neoliberalist doctrine dehumanises in order to exploit the individual. Human beings are understood to be resources similar to coal or iron ore. Institutions, including large Catholic organisations, in defying their own Catholic intellectual tradition, have created "Human Resources" departments specifically designed and inspired by market forces, using language and polices to dehumanise. Students, staff, families, the sick, elderly, mentally ill, and so on are described as clients or customers; institutions commodifying relationships, buying and selling people.

> It is not enough to increase the general fund of wealth and then distribute it more fairly. It is not enough to develop technology so that the earth may become a more suitable living place for human beings. The mistakes of those who led the way should help those now on the road to development to avoid certain dangers. The reign of technology—technocracy, as it is called—can cause as much harm to the world of tomorrow as liberalism did to the world of yesteryear. Economics and technology are meaningless if they do not benefit humanity, for it is humanity they are to serve.[23]

Fundamentalisms as a signpost to the Post-Secular Age

The emerging phenomenon of post-secularism is experienced in the increasing connection between the 'two cities,' the temporal-political and the faith-mystical. Elaine Graham acknowledges that the paradoxical co-existence of the religious and the secular in our cultural context, 'takes us into uncharted territory, sociologically and theologically, and has given rise to talk of the emergence of a post-secular society.'[24]

The secular narrative outlined above exists, paradoxically, alongside resurgence in religious consciousness, an awareness that leads some

---
[23] *Populorum Progressio*, 34.
[24] Graham, *Between A Rock and a Hard Place* (2013), xvi.

scholars to argue that this reality is evidence not of the steady decline of religion but its dramatic and often radical resurgence.[25] Religion in one form or another, usually negative, with casual reference to God, continues to capture our attention and is seldom absent from the 24/7 news cycle. Despite the increasing volume of literature inspired by Habermas's notion of post-secularity, there remains little agreement as to the validity of his hypothesis. Habermas pointed to three factors of post-secularity: (i) global conflicts changing public consciousness; (ii) religion gaining influence as it forms communities of interpretation in the public arena and (iii) immigration.[26] Religious observance by definition is not a private affair, arguably today it appears overwhelmingly to consist of a turn to the subjective self.[27] Sources of 'truth', including religious, are multiform, in a similar manner to 'truth' conveyance in contemporary society is multiform.

The concept of post-secular arguably can only be applied to affluent European societies and countries such as New Zealand, Canada and Australia.[28] Positive characteristics of a post-secular milieu might include:

> a renewed interest in the (religious) spiritual life; a relaxation of the secular suspicion towards spiritual questions; a recognition that secular rights and freedoms of expression are a prerequisite to the renewal of spiritual enquiry; a spiritual and intellectual pluralism, East and West; a cherishing of the best in all spiritual traditions, East and West, while recognising the repression sometimes inflicted on individuals or societies in the name of religion.'[29]

---

[25] Graham, *Between A Rock And A Hard Place.*
[26] See Jürgen Habermas, *The Future of Human Nature*, (Cambridge: Polity Press, 2003); 'Religion in the Public Sphere', *European Journal of Philosophy*, (2006), 14:1,1-25; Habermas, *Europe: The Faltering Project*, (Cronin, Ciaran. Trans. Malden, MA: Polity Press, 2009), 84; Habermas, 'What is Meant by a 'Post-Secular Society'? A Discussion on Islam in Europe'. In Habermas, *Europe: The Faltering Project*, 2009; Habermas, et al., *An Awareness of What is Missing: Faith and Reason in a Post-Secular Age*, (Cronin, Ciaran. Trans. Malden, MA: Polity Press, 2010).
[27] Fred Dallmayr, Review of *International Studies* / Volume 38 / Issue 05 / December 2012, 963-973.
[28] See Peter Nynas, Mika Labsauder and Terhi Utriainen (eds), *Post-Secular Society*, (New Jersey: Tranaction Publishers, 2015).
[29] Mike King, Centre for Post-secular Studies, postsecularhttp://www.jnani.org/postsecular/definitions.htm. Accessed July 20, 2016.

An intellectual assent to religious faith in late modernity requires comprehension of the philosophical and cultural turn to the self. Such ascent strives to hold in tension historical consciousness and cultural relativism, the latter dramatically described by Benedict XVI, as a 'dictatorship of relativism'.

With the possible exception of North Korea and China, global and local social-political events, including their recording in our history books, no longer originate from an authoritative, often singular source or group of experts. Examples of past cultural sources of 'truth', such as the BBC, government, religious gurus, academia, the Magisterium, even News Limited no longer have a monopoly on truth. Some world leaders openly challenge the role of experts in society and present "alternative facts" or "fake news" leading to our age being described as "post-truth". It is not unreasonable to argue that the quest for *truth* no longer sells newspapers or influences the election of presidents. It's not so much that 'we can't handle the truth', but rather we have become accustomed to its manipulation by powerful elites. We have evolved to turn inwards to answer questions of truth, and simply prefer our own forms of truth, resisting former sources of authority, thus opinionated rhetoric has in many cases overtaken recourse to fact. News, information, data, opinion are "out there", from numerous sources, so we all form an opinion. Increasingly such *opinion* is the dominant form of truth accepted in Western political culture.

Many in the secular public square continue to question whether religion is a force for good or ill. Jürgen Habermas offers a further seminal contribution to the discussion regarding the positive re-emergence of religion into the public space. He considers religion as a force for good and the identification of modernisation with secularisation as too simplistic. Habermas considered the public space to be 'a discrete, modern dimension of social and political life characterised by communication through participation'. Writing in 2008, he continued, the public space is characterised by 'rational and transformational discourse'. Sadly, just eight years later, and with the emergence of Trump and his twitter machine of self-proclaimed 'truthful hyperbole', employed by an increasing number of western politicians, it seems increasingly difficult to characterise the public space as 'rational discourse'.

On a positive note, Habermas advocates for the enrichment of the public space by 'incorporating what's missing, namely religious values into a renewed vocabulary of civic discourse'. Moving away from his earlier Marxist convictions, Habermas maintains that religious reasoning can and must be introduced into 'the flows of public communication since they 'constitute powerful sources for the creation of meaning and identity'. For Habermas, the reintroduction of religious reasoning, religious values, will lead to 'a renewed vocabulary of civic virtue' and 'constitute powerful and irreducible sources of the creation of meaning and identity'.

More optimistically, and representing the concept of 'post-secularism' in a positive light, as a voice of religious hope and reason, Pope Francis projects a compassionate image of religion into the public space. The Pope is also responsible for increasing religious consciousness on a global scale. Most recently, he appeared on the cover of *Time* magazine and was considered by a Win/Gallup poll the world's most popular leader. Taking on the name of a humble saint and calling the Church to work for healing, he is currently on the world stage being the voice of the voiceless, advocating for the rights of refugees and seeking compassion for the marginalised around the globe.

Also moving into the world of politics, Francis is currently working as a mediator between the Venezuelan government and the opposition to help achieve a resolution to the current political crisis in South America. Holding news headlines around the world during the 2016 American presidential campaign, Francis urged Donald Trump and all world leaders, to build bridges to bring peoples together rather than walls which divide. In the thought of Francis, religion can bring peoples together in a movement towards a moral universalism that recognises the dignity of each human being. A religious movement of this nature, generated by Francis, may encourage western culture to see the dignity of humanity as the sacred goal of our age.

The election of Donald Trump gives evidence to this new radical "post-truth" world in which truth is understood to be a matter of opinion. The good, the true, are in danger of becoming little more than a feeling, or what Trump described, when a particular falsehood became public, "truthful hyperbole". In our scientific age, devoid of a philosophical-theology at the heart of its secular universities, the fruit of the enlightenment might well be that facts and evidence are no longer of central concern. Climate change deniers regardless of the overwhelming scientific evidence, are a concerning example of an emerging phenomena. Theology needs to be at the heart of the university. All religions should desire to be at the heart of secular universities, to engage in mutually enriching dialogue with science and the arts, particularly the human sciences. Without such transparent and rigorous critique, religion will ever be prone to the abuse of fundamentalism.

Conclusion: Christianity at the Crossroads of Post Modernity Requires Refounding

Undoubtedly, dramatic but no less true, the future of humanity and the planet rests upon authentic dialogue and partnership between peoples, nations, religions and cultures. [30] Reminiscent of the great Hebrew prophets from ancient times, Martin Luther King's *Dream* gave the world a pathway to walk, an insight into the potential hope-filled gifts that Christianity can propose to all humanity.

> I have a dream that one day every valley shall be exalted, every hill and mountain shall be made low, the rough places will be made plain, and the crooked places will be made straight, and the glory of the Lord shall be revealed, and all flesh shall see it together... This is our hope... with this faith we will be able to hew out of the mountain of despair a stone of hope... Let freedom ring from every hill...with this faith we will be able to transform the jangling discords... into a beautiful symphony of [sister and] brotherhood.[31]

---

[30] See Gerald A. Arbuckle, *Catholic Identity or Identities? Refounding Ministries in Chaotic Times*, (Collegeville, Minnesota: Liturgical Press, 2013) 99, and *Evangelii Gaudium*, 11.
[31] Martin Luther King, 'I have A Dream', speech delivered during the March on Washington for Jobs and Freedom on August 28, 1963.

Christianity can present itself to the world at the crossroads of post-modernity with joy and hope, singing the Lord's song in a strange land, an "open" aria to the pursuit of truth. A search for truth that is cognisant of and in partnership with other songs that also seek truth. As *Lumen Gentium* (Light to the Nations) wisely taught, 'all mankind, [are] called by God's grace to salvation', all cultures and religions have gifts to share for the good of humanity.[32] The bishops and theologians in drafting *Lumen Gentium* presented an inclusive open truth narrative:

> ...the plan of salvation also includes those who acknowledge the Creator, in the first place amongst whom are the Moslems: these profess to hold the faith of Abraham, and together with us they adore the one, merciful God, mankind's judge on the last day. Nor is God remote from those who in shadows and images seek the unknown God, since he gives to all men (and women) life and breath and all things (cf. Acts 17:25-28), and since the Saviour wills all men to be saved (cf. 1 Tim. 2:4). Those who, through no fault of their own, do not know the Gospel of Christ or his Church, but who nevertheless seek God with a sincere heart, and, moved by grace, try in their actions to do his will as they know it through the dictates of their conscience - those too many achieve eternal salvation. Nor shall divine providence deny the assistance necessary for salvation to those who, without any fault of theirs, have not yet arrived at an explicit knowledge of God, and who, not without grace, strive to lead a good life.[33]

From an anthropological perspective, if a culture is to succeed, then it has to develop mechanisms enabling people who are different to live together in a way that treats difference as a graced resource and not as a limitation.

> The reality is that cultures of any kind, if left unchecked, in their effort to maintain order can suffocate diversities; creativity ceases and people die as human persons.[34]

---

[32] *Lumen Gentium*, 13.
[33] *Lumen Gentium*, 16.
[34] Gerald A. Arbuckle, *The Francis Factor and the People of God: New Life for the Church*, (Maryknoll, NY: Orbis Books, 2015), 91-160.

Humanity is fully human only if we are master of our own actions (conscience) and act according to our God-given nature, freely accepting its potentials and its claims upon us. Christianity can offer to post-modernity a theological anthropology based upon the dignity of the human person *(Cura Personalis)*, including: a contemporary understanding of evil, the fall of Adam and Original Sin. Christianity's ability to articulate and practice *Cura Personalis* in a multifaith, multicultural, postmodern context, will determine the future nature of the church.[35]

The Jesuit Pedro Arrupe, another inspiring example of a refounding prophet, and considered by many to be the most influential Catholic churchman of the twentieth century, arguably refounded the Society of Jesus.

Refounding people who, in imitation of the shock the original founding person experienced on perceiving the gap between deeply held values and the world of their time, acutely sees a like chasm between these values and their contemporary reality, and moves, through creative strategies, to bridge the gulf. While at the same time, restlessly summoning others to undergo a similar conversion, to share in the vision, and to venture into the unknown in order to implement the strategies.[36]

In a similar manner, another Jesuit, Pope Francis, is continuing the undertaking of a refounding of the Catholic Church. He has unparalleled support (Reception) from the People of God.[37] His theological method, like Arrupe's, is based upon a theological anthropology and a diachronic and synchronic *modus operandi* cognisant of a humbled Christianity, (modelled upon the humble servant of Isaiah), and again, situated at the crossroads of post modernity.

---

[35] *Cura Personalis* relates to Ignatian spirituality and translates as 'care of the whole person', suggestive of individualised attention to the needs of others, along with distinct respect for unique circumstances and concerns and an appropriate appreciation for singular gifts and insights. Cf. *'Cura Personalis'*, Peter-Hans Kolvenbach S.J., *Review of Ignatian Spirituality*, 9-17. http://www.sjweb.info/documents/cis/pdfenglish/200711402en.pdf. Accessed July 20, 2016.

[36] Gerald A Arbuckle, *Refounding the Church: Dissent for Leadership* (New York: Orbis Books, 1993), 147.

[37] See Chapter Two, *Lumen Gentium*, 'The People of God'.

Pope Francis by his actions and words is breaking through years of scandals, cultural trauma and impasse, allowing the people of God to mourn openly and to hope for newness based on the mythology of Vatican II. As a ritual leader of mourning he is refounding the church, seeking to draw others to join him in this collaborative process.[38]

A Christianity based on the model of refounding may be identified as a movement unobstructed by internally or externally constructed denominational borders or walls. As such, an ecumenically minded church may be understood to be on pilgrimage, living at peace with a secular open-truth world view.[39] A Christianity that brings about the Reign of God will self-identify as a dialogical church, though being mission orientated and engaged in 'refounding' of Christianity. A refounding Christianity will experience an ecumenical church, one living at peace with its own internal diversity and with an outward looking external embrace of secular culture.

A refounding of church is based upon a recontextualisation, together with an appropriation of the human sciences, allowing Christianity to use the resources available in post-modern society to engage with the signs of the times. Our time is characterised in part by growing division within societies and international relations, a separatism that breeds fundamentalisms. A refounding church, accompanied by a 'dying' of the old hegemonic powers, requires a refounding of the dignity of the human person *(Cura Personalis)*, particularly the emancipation of the oppressed. Such a position would represent in an ecclesial context a world-view articulated through the language of a liberated theology, and a subsequent Liberation Theology. An outlook cognisant of and in dialogue with multi-directional pathways authentically represents a way of faith inspired by the non-hegemonic and generative teachings of Jesus Christ.

---

[38] Gerald A. Arbuckle, *The Francis Factor and the People of God: New Life for the* Church (Maryknoll, NY: Orbis Books, 2015), 197-98.

[39] See Gerald A. Arbuckle, *Out of Chaos: Refounding Religious Congregations* (London: Geoffrey Chapman, 1988), pp.94-95, 163-64; *The Francis Factor and the People of God: New Life for the Church* (Maryknoll, NY: Orbis Books, 2015), 147-50.

The result would be a more culturally relevant Christianity with a refounding mission activated by the Holy Spirit. Through God's grace, liberation gifts the virtues (faith, hope, love, courage, wisdom, justice, mercy and so forth) empowering bishops and theologians to speak the language of post-modern culture. As a father of four culturally switched on kids, I have learnt from them that the Church presents a too often medieval philosophical face to the world. The church too often speaks a closed meta-narrative that has been firmly and universally rejected by our university and "life" educated post-critical young people. In reality, the Church struggles theologically to support post-critical young people, or their parents, in nurturing a post-modern Catholic faith. At best, many of our young people, who are well versed in the achievements of scientific age, understand the Church to be a Jurassic Park. They see a church trapped in time, (a closed meta-narrative), an aged-care facility for dinosaurs enclosed behind high walls that obscure the speeding meteor of post-modernity which is already upon them.

Proponents of the three closed meta-narratives under discussion in this chapter each claim to hold the one truth. Their story is presented as the only story. They assert their monopoly on truth to the detriment of reason, history, logic or fact. In contrast, a refounding Christianity will be a church built upon the Christian virtues of love, humility, hospitality, hope and courage, and the abdication of hegemonic power. By definition, a church at the crossroads of post-modernity will have jettisoned a closed meta-narrative, in a concerted effort to get to that place of dialogue with the other, seeking truth and embracing on the journey the value of diversity.

A refounding Christianity will move beyond Gramsci's interregnum, allowing the old to die naturally and the new to be born. A refounding Christianity will be ever more cognisant of Lyotard's advice not to build walls of closed-truth (religious, atheist and neoliberal) meta-narratives. A refounding Christianity will be mindful of the ageless underground class warfare evident in the church and society. Class conflict has once more emerged into the light of history and is both illustrated and exacerbated by the Global Financial Crisis and the economic disparity between countries of the North and South.

So many of the world's poor, the majority of humanity, are now aware (through communication technology) of the economic disparity and seek equality, some seek revenge. Those in hegemonic positions of power and privilege are equally cognisant of global injustice, a growing number are engaging in work of restorative justice.

Finally, this chapter aspires to make a contribution to the task of practical theology. Practical Theology by definition is to be situated in the public square, to advocate for global dialogue and consensus around the dignity of the human person. In essence this eschatological endeavour requires challenging all forms of closed truth fundamentalisms, including the competing secular claims with regard to the materialistic nature of reality.[40] Theology then is called into the public midst, to witness to an open-truth narrative. At the crossroads of post modernity, such earnest endeavour might just possibly begin to inspire a new generation of post-critical young people to engage in a post-secular refounding of church and society. A refounding characterised through *petits récits*, and an invitation to sing again the Lord's song in a not too strange land.

---

[40] See Gerald A. Arbuckle, *Culture, Inculturation, and Theologians: A Postmodern Critique* (Collegeville, MN: Liturgical Press, 2010), 138-88; *Catholic Identity or Identities? Refounding Ministries in Chaotic Times,* (Collegeville, MN: Liturgical Press, 2013).

Chapter Two

Speaking Christian: Toward a Post-secular Apologetics

Elaine Graham

Introduction

In this chapter I want to talk about the return of religion to public consciousness, but not in ways to which we may necessarily have been accustomed. After generations in which the assumptions of classical secularisation theory[1] governed discussions of the place of religion in public life, we find ourselves having to come to terms not with the steady decline of religion but its dramatic and often disturbing resurgence. Yet what makes this situation even more complex is that whilst this 'new visibility' of religion is unavoidable, the trajectory of religious revival often collides with the forces of resilient and enduring secularism. The latter still remains the default position for much public debate, certainly in Western post-industrial societies, for whom the continued decline of organised religion still forms the backdrop for relationships between Church and state, politics and faith. This is therefore a situation which fits neither a narrative of secularisation nor one of restoration. In everyday terms, we witness this paradoxical situation in the ways society is nervous about those who 'do God' in public, since it is unused to thinking about whether it is right to (re) incorporate the vocabulary of faith into our common life; and yet, we see how religion is an ever-present reality and often manifests itself in new, unfamiliar – sometimes banal, sometimes shocking - ways and spaces, local and global. Public life is more sensitive – if not necessarily well-informed – about newly-emergent signs of religious

---

[1] Steve Bruce, *Secularisation: In Defence of an Unfashionable Theory* (Oxford: Oxford University Press, 2010).

belief and practice in its midst, yet often struggles to accommodate it into any meaningful framework.

As a result, it may be more illuminating to think of ourselves as occupying a new space, somewhere between the renewed visibility of religion in public life, with its (somewhat reluctant) recognition of the importance of religious values and actors on the one hand, and the persistence of widespread scepticism towards religion on the other. With its enduring expressions of secular objections to religion as a source of legitimate public discourse [2], my main aim here is to consider some of its implications, not least for the public witness of Christianity. If the gulf between those who identify themselves as practising members of faith-communities and the rest of the community is widening, what conventions now govern the terms on which religion can participate in the public square? Is faith the answer or part of the problem? Whose responsibility is it to govern the terms of engagement across the post-secular divide; and what kinds of measures might contribute towards some kind of *rapprochement*? How do those who are appointed as representatives of religious institutions claim any legitimacy for their participation in an increasingly fragmented political culture? What is an appropriately Christian response to these questions, and is it possible to articulate a faithful praxis of public engagement for a post-secular era?

In such a situation, I am going to suggest that what may be needed is a reorientation of traditions of public theology towards a kind of Christian apologetics. Apologetics refers to the perennial task for the Church of offering a reasoned defence or rationale for its faith. It may be defined, after Avery Dulles, as 'the various ways in which thoughtful Christians, in different ages and cultures, have striven to 'give a reason for the hope that is within them' (cf 1 Peter 3.15)'[3]. Christianity is essentially a missionary faith, centred from its earliest beginnings upon a proclamation of the life, death, resurrection and Lordship of

---

[2] Jürgen Habermas *et al.*, *An Awareness of what is Missing: Faith and Reason in a Post-Secular Age* (Cambridge: Polity, 2010); Elaine Graham, *Between a Rock and a Hard Place: Public Theology in a Post-Secular Age* (London: SCM Press, 2013); James Beckford, 'Public Religions and the Postsecular: Critical Reflections', *Journal for the Scientific Study of Religion*, 51.1 (2012): 1-19.

[3] Avery Dulles, *A History of Apologetics* (First published 1971). (Eugene, ON: Wipf and Stock, 1999), xix.

Jesus Christ. Yet coupled with that has also been an apologetic task, whereby the Church has had to defend and commend its claims against a variety of fellow-travellers, detractors and secular authorities: Jews, pagans, sceptics and Emperors.[4]

Avery Dulles has described the contemporary apologist as 'an aggressive, opportunistic person who tries, by fair means or foul, to argue people into joining the church'[5] (1971, p. xv). But that adversarial, often very abstract, style of argumentation is, I'll argue, a departure from much of Christian history, which regarded apologetics less as a fight to the death over Christian doctrine, so much as a demonstration in deed as well as word of how the practice of faith makes a difference. It is an invitation to inhabit a shared space of dialogue and exchange in the spirit of hospitality, rather than competition. In many respects, the ways in which contemporary public theologians are charged to 'speak truth to power' and mediate insights from Christian thought and practice into a secular, pluralist public square has much in common with that tradition; and so I want to develop that convergence by asking what it would mean for public theology to undertake – or reclaim – the practice of apologetics for a post-secular society.

The Anatomy of the Post-Secular new visibility of religion

Where does the debate about the post-secular originate? The sociologist Peter Berger has famously summarised the problem in these terms:

> ... the assumption that we live in a secularised world is false. The world today, with some exceptions ... is as furiously religious as it ever was, and in some places more so than ever. This means that a whole body of literature by historians and social scientists loosely labelled 'secularisation theory' is essentially mistaken.[6]

---

[4] Graham, *Between a Rock and a Hard Place*, 179.
[5] Dulles, (1999), *History of Apologetics*, xv.
[6] Peter Berger, 'The Desecularisation of the World: a Global Overview', in *The Desecularisation of the World: Resurgent Religion and World Politics*, edited by Peter Berger (Grand Rapids, MN: Wm B Eerdmans, 1999): 1-18, 2.

For most of the second half of the twentieth century in Europe, North America, Australia and New Zealand, the gradual marginalisation of religious belief and institutions and the privatisation of religious belief and practice formed the mainstay of social scientific thinking about religion. The dynamics of secularisation were, of course, a matter of debate; but broadly the consensus was that it wove together a number of threads. First, it traced the gradual separation or differentiation of religious institutions (such as the Christian church in the West) from mainstream society – so for example, the removal of education, welfare, morality, even rites of passage from the hands of religious institutions into those of the State. Secondly, it mapped the process of declining participation and belief in religious practices and dogmas on an individual level; and thirdly, it predicted the general privatisation of religion within the moral, cultural and intellectual life of any society.

Where I think the situation in the twenty-first century differs, and where it confounds the sociological orthodoxy of the mid- to late-twentieth, however, is the unexpected and unprecedented re-emergence of religion onto the global political scene. One of the characteristics of the past thirty years has been the way in which religion has become newly visible and experienced as a global phenomenon of considerable political and cultural power - for good and ill. Globally, of course, the rise of radical Islam, especially in the Middle East, East Asia and Africa, and of Hindu nationalism in India, represent examples of the ways in which, far from receding to the margins of our political consciousness, has now erupted with unprecedented force. As Table 1 indicates, globally speaking the world's population is still, and will probably continue to be, largely religious.

Table 1: Comparative projections of major religious groups, 2010-50

Size and Projected Growth of Major Religious Groups

	2010 POPULATION	% OF WORLD POPULATION IN 2010	PROJECTED 2050 POPULATION	% OF WORLD POPULATION IN 2050	POPULATION GROWTH 2010-2050
Christians	2,168,330,000	31.4%	2,918,070,000	31.4%	749,740,000
Muslims	1,599,700,000	23.2	2,761,480,000	29.7	1,161,780,000
Unaffiliated	1,131,150,000	16.4	1,230,340,000	13.2	99,190,000
Hindus	1,032,210,000	15.0	1,384,360,000	14.9	352,140,000
Buddhists	487,760,000	7.1	486,270,000	5.2	-1,490,000
Folk Religions	404,690,000	5.9	449,140,000	4.8	44,450,000
Other Religions	58,150,000	0.8	61,450,000	0.7	3,300,000
Jews	13,860,000	0.2	16,090,000	0.2	2,230,000
World total	6,895,850,000	100.0	9,307,190,000	100.0	2,411,340,000

Source: The Future of World Religions: Population Growth Projections, 2010-2050
PEW RESEARCH CENTER

Sadly, the events of the shootings at the *Charlie Hebdo* offices in Paris in January 2015 were a graphic demonstration of the tensions between the Muslim world and Western powers that has emerged as one of the defining fault-lines of global politics.[7] And whilst there are several mitigating factors behind those divisions, a perception on the part of many Muslims that one of the things that distinguishes them from the West is a way of life that is fundamentally religious, is clearly primary. It also highlights, in passing, the fact that Europe (to a lesser extent North America and parts of Oceania) may actually be a secularised 'exception' to an otherwise mainly religious world.

This trend also runs against the grain of much sociological orthodoxy in that this new visibility of religion and its vitality – certainly in the global South - is fully associated with the processes and technologies of globalised capitalism, immigration and urbanisation. In other words, it is not the conventional sociological narrative of religion (representing the forces of affect, tradition, organic community, nature) being irrevocably eclipsed by modernising forces (representing the triumph of reason, innovation, science, technology). The current situation is therefore unprecedented historically.

---

[7] Didier Fassin, 'In the Name of the Republic: untimely meditations on the aftermath of the Charlie Hebdo attack', *Anthropology Today*, 31.2 (2015): 3-7.

But even within the West, where the decline of institutional Christianity (but not that of other faiths) may still bear out much of twentieth-century secularisation theory, religion is reasserting its visibility within the political discourses shaping fundamental debates about the social order, as well as colonising new spaces and generating new alliances and social movements. Ironically, austerity measures on the part of many governments following the global economic crisis of 2008-9 have furnished many faith-based organisations such as churches with opportunities to 'push back against the pressures of secularisation'[8] by offering buildings, resources and volunteers as statutory facilities are withdrawn. There are other dimensions to this new visibility too which buck the trend of secularising narratives. For example, evidence consistently reports that those who participate in religious activities record higher levels of well-being and mental health, prompting renewed interest in the clinical benefits of religious and spiritual practices even within secular, clinical agencies.[9]

Continuing Decline

Yet whilst religion may be newly visible - and often troubling - to Western liberal ideals of a neutral public square, its resurgent forms are very different from anything resembling a return to Christendom such as existed in medieval and early modern Europe. The religious landscape is far more diverse and complex. For a start, levels of formal institutional affiliation and membership in mainstream Christian (and Jewish) denominations continue to diminish across the Western world. Table 2 highlights some dimensions of this decline.

---

[8] Steven Kettell, 'Illiberal Secularism? Pro-faith discourse in the United Kingdom', *Is God Back? Reconsidering the new visibility of religion*, (editor) Titus Hjelm (London: Bloomsbury, 2015): 65-76, 69.
[9] Jonathan Rowson, 'Love, Death, Self and Soul', *RSA Journal* 4.4 (2014): 48.

Table 2: Continuing Trajectories of Secularisation

Countries That Will No Longer Have a Christian Majority in 2050

	MAJORITY RELIGION 2010	% OF POPULATION 2010	MAJORITY/LARGEST RELIGION 2050	% OF POPULATION 2050
Australia	Christians	67.3%	Christians	47.0%
United Kingdom	Christians	64.3	Christians	45.4
Benin	Christians	53.0	Christians	48.5
France	Christians	63.0	Unaffiliated	44.1
Republic of Macedonia	Christians	59.3	Muslims	56.2
New Zealand	Christians	57.0	Unaffiliated	45.1
Bosnia-Herzegovina	Christians	52.3	Muslims	49.4
Netherlands	Christians	50.6	Unaffiliated	49.1

Source: The Future of World Religions: Population Growth Projections, 2010-2050
PEW RESEARCH CENTER

But even 'faith' itself, certainly within a Western Christian context, cannot easily be mapped back onto the old churchgoing patterns of the 1950s. Even if forms of organised religion do still hold sway, they are far more deinstitutionalised and fluid due to social media, globalisation and post-traditional forms of church. People are more likely to describe themselves as 'Spiritual but not Religious'.[10] Statistics on the religious outlooks and affiliations of young people suggest these tendencies are intensifying as one generation succeeds another.[11] A Pew Research Center survey in the US in 2010 recorded 25 per cent of adults born after 1980 (so-called 'Generation Y', or under 30s) as unaffiliated, describing their religion as 'atheist,' 'agnostic' or 'nothing in particular.' This compares with less than one-fifth of people in their 30s (Generation X, at 19 per cent), 15 per cent of those in their 40s, 14 per cent of those in their 50s and 10 per cent or less among those 60 and older.[12]

---
[10] Robert Fuller, *Spiritual but not Religious* (Oxford: Oxford University Press, 2001).
[11] ComRes, *The Spirit of Things Unseen Spirituality Survey* (London: Theos, 2013); Mathew Guest, Kristin Aune, Sonya Sharma and Robert Warner, *Christianity and the University Experience* (London: Bloomsbury, 2013); 'Pew Forum on Religion and Public Life', *Religion among the Millennials* (Washington, DC: Pew Research Center, 2010).
[12] Pew Forum, (2010) *Religion among the Millennials*.

Table 3: The Rise of the 'Nones'

Rapid Growth in Number of Religious 'Nones' Who Say Religion Is Not Important to Them

	2007	2014	Change
Number of adults in U.S.	227.2m	244.8m	+17.6m
Share of adults who are religiously unaffiliated	16.1%	22.8%	+6.7 points
NUMBER of religiously unaffiliated adults	36.6m	55.8m	+19.2m
Share of unaffiliated adults saying religion is "not too/not at all" important in their lives	57.5%	64.7%	+7.2 points
NUMBER of religiously unaffiliated adults saying religion is not important in their lives	**21.0m**	**36.1m**	**+15.1m**

Source: 2014 Religious Landscape Study, conducted June 4-Sept. 30, 2014.
PEW RESEARCH CENTER

The prevailing mood in the West according to the logic of the post-secular might therefore be summarised as follows:

> Not hostile to or uninformed about Christianity, often interested in spiritual questions and prepare to face the difficult issues of mortality and meaning. And yet the Church is the last place they would look for answers.[13]

Resistance to Religion as Reasonable Public Discourse

But perhaps the most serious finding of recent research, and one which is quite relevant to our concerns, is the conclusion that religion is viewed increasingly within public opinion not as something innocuous or marginal, but, as Linda Woodhead has put it, 'a toxic brand'[14]. So the post-secular contains a mix of growth and decline, religious pluralism and diversification, serving to confound many of the secular premises of Western modernity, one aspect to endure is widespread cultural suspicion of and resistance to religion as a public phenomenon. And whilst a lot of that probably only manifests itself at this instinctive distrust of organised, dogmatic faith, it is important to acknowledge

---

[13] Graham Tomlin, *The Provocative Church* (3rd Edition), (London: SPCK, 2008): 4.
[14] Jessica Elgot, 'Half of Brits Say Religion Does More Harm Than Good, and Atheists Can Be Just as Moral', <http://www.huffingtonpost.co.uk/2014/11/03/religion-beyond-belief_n_6094442.html>. Accessed 11 October 2015.

the impact on public discourse of the continued popularity of a group of high-profile atheist and humanists who consistently voice objections to the very legitimacy of religion as a form of public discourse.

In 2008-2009, a federation of secularists and atheists in the UK sponsored a red London bus emblasoned with the slogan, 'There's probably no god. Now get on and enjoy your life.' This was a campaign on behalf of that philosophical perspective which can trace its influences back to the eighteenth century European and North American Enlightenment with its elevation of reason and human self-determination, and which regards religion as antipathetic to such ideals. Religion is a sorry vestige of the past, perpetuating our subservience to supernatural powers, rather than promoting a faith in human potential, progress and the benefits of science. They are the heirs of scientific rationalism who regard faith as nonsensical, deluded and dangerous, a dangerous infantile dependency on superstation. Michael DeLashmutt summarises their position in this way: 'Religion is bad for you. God is a deluded fantasy. Get rid of faith and grow up.'[15] Their objections to religion may also be on moral grounds, regarding religion an implacable and pathological source of violence, abuse and autocratic authority.[16]

For New Atheists, the end of God is the beginning of human freedom. Religion is inherently irrational, infantile and abusive. Such campaigners object to any religiously-motivated intervention in public life, such as policies around same-sex marriage, assisted dying, faith schools, and so on. And in that scepticism, we see tangible evidence for a greater complexity beyond Berger's use of the term 'desecularisation'[17]. Rather than simple reversal, we are witnessing the extended after-life of the secularisation thesis, coupled with the mutation and diversification of many forms of religious practice, both formal and historic, as well as innovative and more personalised.

---

[15] Michael DeLashmutt, 'Delusions and Dark Materials: New Atheism as Naive Atheism and its Challenge to Theological Education', *Expository Times* 120:12 (2009): 586-593, 589.
[16] Sam Harris, *The End of Faith: Religion, Terror, and the Future of Reason* (London: Free Press, 2005).
[17] Berger, (1999), 'The Desecularisation of the World'.

This new unexpected turn in the story of secularisation has had a profound effect on many intellectuals within political philosophy and social theory as well as the study of religion. Assumptions that an inevitable consequence of economic modernisation right across all cultures would mean the disappearance of religion have had to be revised. In political theory at least, this meant the revision of a liberal-democratic model premised on the separation of religious conviction (deemed private) and a neutral body politic (the realm of the public) in which 'talk of God' and allusions to the sacred were deemed inadmissible.

Writers such as Talal Asad have made connections between this interruption in the flow of the secularisation narrative and the emergence of post-colonial critiques of Western ways of thinking. The very concept of secularisation, and the binary logic of sacred and secular, hinged on Western readings of history and culture.[18] So the revision of this thesis was, partly, a recognition that a particular conceptual framework didn't fit; and partly a realisation that global events were moving in new, unexpected directions. The norm, and the centre of gravity, is much closer to cultures of the global South, which have never really been 'secular' in terms of the modern, liberal separation of religion and politics.

Yet at the same time, exceptionalism apart, for those in the West it is undeniably the case that even where there are signs of re-emergent religious belief and practice, they occur within a context that we experience as radically and irrevocably secular. As Charles Taylor has argued, even those of a strong personal faith conviction recognise the existence of pluralism of belief and non-belief, such that any kind of committed religious identity is a choice. At one point in his book, *A Secular Age*, Taylor talks about the 'Unquiet Frontiers of Modernity'[19], to describe how it feels to inhabit a world seemingly far removed from religion, which is nevertheless profoundly shot through with glimpses of what he calls 'a place of fullness'.[20] As moderns, we have learned

---

[18] Talal Asad, *Formations of the Secular: Christianity, Islam, Modernity* (Stanford, CA: Stanford University Press, 2003).
[19] Charles Taylor, *A Secular Age* (Cambridge, MA: Belknapp Press/Harvard University Press, 2007), 711-727.
[20] Taylor, (2007), *A Secular Age*, 6.

to be self-sufficient, to live immanent lives and yet at the periphery of our vision, our lived quotidian experience, lies a different landscape, in which our horizons of meaning, belonging and identity hint at a transcendent source, beyond immanence, which speaks of 'some good higher than, beyond human flourishing.'[21] We have, if you like, then, crossed a 'post-secular' Rubicon into a world still ambivalent about religion but one that is increasingly and often unexpectedly receptive to it. Westerners cannot *not* live, on a day-to-day basis, often quite unconsciously, within the 'immanent frame' of secularity.[22]

So as far as many parts of the world are concerned, the post-secular speaks of resurgence and mutation rather than revival. Religious belief and practice in all its forms is seeking to establish new profiles within a public realm that is itself both more globally integrated and more fragmented and diverse. In such context, the legitimacy of religious discourse and practice within the public domain will be welcomed by some as representing a constructive good, whilst vigorously contested by others. Terry Eagleton pithily summarises the conflicted and paradoxical nature of the post-secular in this way:

> No sooner had a thoroughly atheistic culture arrived on the scene ... than the deity himself was suddenly back on the agenda with a vengeance. ... The world is ... divided between those who believe too much and those who believe too little.[23]

However fractured and fragmented the public domain may be, however, the re-emergence of religion as a force in public life requires the voices of faith to consider how best to communicate the basis for their convictions.

> No longer is [the Church] speaking into a common frame of reference, in which [its] theological and moral allusions fall comfortably on waiting ears. The post-secular describes a public square that is both more sensitive to and suspicious of religious discourse. Indeed, in a context where people's familiarity with any kind of organised religion is ever more tenuous, it places greater onus than ever on the importance of significant communication across the post-secular divide.[24]

---

[21] Taylor, (2007), *A Secular Age*, 20.
[22] Taylor, (2007), *A Secular Age*, 20.
[23] Terry Eagleton, *Culture and the Death of God* (New Haven: Yale University Press, 2014), 197.
[24] Graham, (2013), *Between a Rock and a Hard Place*, xx.

Whilst the church struggles to make space in our culture today to be heard, this calls for a creative and proactive engagement with our culture. It requires those of us who are public theologians to acknowledge the reasons why people find religion alien and 'toxic' and to engage seriously with that. Out of that awareness that nothing can be taken for granted, that the world at large no longer feels at ease with religion and cannot understand when the churches 'speak Christian', then we need to search for the points of engagement and dialogue all the more diligently. How is this to be done?

I want to consider whether part of that undertaking for public theology might be to recover an *apologetic* dimension for itself. As a practice old and new, it suggests itself as a way of articulating theological norms for Christians who are concerned to engage constructively with public debate and contemporary culture, who are aware of the growing gulf between that and religious faith, and yet who still want to communicate the basis of their convictions and the roots of their concern for the well-being of society convincingly and reasonably to the world at large.

Public theology varies across different contexts, but has a number of core features. Broadly, it seeks to comment and critically reflect from a theological perspective on aspects of public life such as economics, politics, culture and media. Traditionally, the notion of 'public' has encompassed several dimensions. First, a commitment to the public, social and structural articulation of religion in the face of its privatisation or withdrawal into forms of personal piety. [25]

Secondly, public theology refers to the ways in which religion interacts with common social questions concerning economics, media, politics, law, globalisation, social justice and the environment. It addresses the moral and social transformation not just of individuals, but powers and principalities, structures and systems. And thirdly, it reflects a pledge *to do one's theology in public:* in other words, to conduct these debates about the religious and spiritual contribution to

---

[25] Max Stackhouse, *God and Globalisation, Volume 4: Globalisation and Grace* (New York: Continuum, 2007); E. Harold Breitenberg Jr., 'To tell the truth: will the real public theology stand up?' *Journal of Society of Christian Ethics* 23.2 (2003): 55-96; Elaine Graham and Stephen Lowe, *What Makes a Good City? Public Theology and the Urban Church* (London: SPCK, 2009).

political and other matters in ways that are transparent and publicly accessible to those beyond the immediate faith community.[26] Public theologians regard themselves as rooted in specific religious traditions, but strongly in conversation with secular discourse and public institutions.

As Max Stackhouse puts it,

> ... if a theology is to be trusted to participate in public discourse it ought to be able to make a plausible case for what it advocates in terms that can be comprehended by those who are not believers ... It should be able to articulate its core convictions in comprehensible terms across many modes of discourse, explaining its symbolic and mythical terms ... in ways that expose their multiple levels of meaning.[27]

This is where I think public theology already carries the seeds of its 'apologetic' imperative.

Christian Apologetics, Ancient and Modern

So public theology faces the challenge not only of articulating theologically grounded interventions in the public square but of justifying and defending the very relevance of the Christian faith to a culture that no longer grants it automatic access or credence. I wonder whether that places us in continuity with the past, with the days before Christendom, since defending and commending the Gospel to a culture largely indifferent or even hostile to it was also one of the tasks with which the earliest Christians were charged.

In his *History of Apologetics*, Avery Dulles identifies three strands of Christian apologetics. '*Religious apologists*' traditionally engaged with adherents of other religious or philosophical systems and debated the intellectual coherence of the Gospel. '*Internal apologists*' were more concerned to address doctrinal error or heresy within the Christian community itself. A third group, which Dulles terms '*Political apologists*' advanced defences of Christianity to the powers-that-be, often in the face of state persecution.[28]

---

[26] Breitenberg, (2003), 'To Tell the Truth'.
[27] Stackhouse, (2007), *God and Globalisation*, 112.
[28] Dulles, (1999), *History of Apologetics*, xx.

So we might say that from the very beginning, the task of apologetics has been one of communicating its claims to a variety of non-believers, adversaries and potential persecutors. The early Christian epistle, the first letter of Peter, summarises this imperative as follows:

> Who is going to harm you if you are eager to do good? But even if you should suffer for what is right, you are blessed. Do not fear what they fear; do not be frightened. But in your hearts, set apart Christ as Lord. Always be prepared to give an answer to everyone who asks you to give the reason for the hope that you have. But do this with gentleness and respect, keeping a clear conscience, so that those who speak maliciously against your good behaviour in Christ may be ashamed of their slander. [29]

Always be prepared to give an answer to everyone who asks you to give the reason for the hope that you have. This is a text forged out of the collective experience of those who perceived themselves as suffering for their faith, which by all accounts was not uncommon amongst first and second century Christian communities. Commentators are unsure as to whether this was chiefly at the hands of the State or simply everyday hostility from those around them.[30] The legal connotations of 'apologia' suggest that the 'account' the Christians are called to give would be in a court of law; but, on the other hand, the imperative to respond to anyone and everyone who asks suggests that it may have been in response to more low-key hostility.[31]

This social and political climate called for a particular kind of resilience, which the writer of Peter argues rests in the example and inspiration of Christ himself. The community is advised to see no contradiction between whatever difficulties they experience in the present and the reward or vindication that is to come, since this mirrors the logic of Christ's suffering and death and the promise of his resurrection. This is the 'hope' that sustains them in their privation.[32] They are encouraged to stand firm in the face of ill-treatment. In spite of their suffering, no real harm can befall the ones who live with integrity and who hold to their faith. Good deeds and upright behaviour are their most effective warrant.

---

[29] 1 Peter 3:13-17, *New International Version*.
[30] David Horrell, *1 Peter* (London: T & T Clark, 2008).
[31] Peter Achtemeier, *1 Peter* (Minneapolis: Fortress Press, 1996), 34-36.
[32] Horrell, (2008), *1 Peter*.

By living distinctive and exemplary lives, neither surrendering to persecution nor assimilating to ungodly values, Christians identify with Christ's redemptive suffering and affirm their hope in the ultimate victory of the Cross. And if to be a 'Christian' is considered a crime, then it is one that a Christian should uphold with pride. This in and of itself might be seen as another small subversion of Imperial authority, since in a normal trial one pleads innocent to any charges - yet here, believers are exhorted to confess freely to their faith in the name of Christ who also underwent trial and punishment. The praxis and witness of a community prepared to model its corporate life on the suffering of Jesus constitutes its own best apologetic.

Elsewhere in the New Testament, we have other notable precedents. Beginning with the day of Pentecost (Acts 2) the disciples communicated the Good News through the medium of their audience's various cultural and linguistic vernaculars. Acts of the Apostles records how Peter's address to the crowd was couched in a way that placed Jesus as Messiah, prophet of Israel and fulfilment of the Hebrew Scriptures (Acts 2:14–36). When in Athens, Paul deliberately adopts the philosophical presuppositions of the crowd at the Aeropagus in order to show how Christ is already prefigured in their culture (Acts 17:16–33). These principles establish important precedents: of beginning from the world-view of one's dialogue partner, with an ability to be 'bilingual'[33] in being able to mediate between the language of faith and the presuppositions of one's audience.

As Christianity itself expanded, so it encountered different alternative cultures, and continued to attract attention, not all of it benign, from the Imperial authorities. Whilst many apologies were philosophical in nature, intended as defences of the logical coherence of Christian theology, many others addressed themselves to the public standing of Christians, protesting against the injustice of the legal charges – ranging from sedition, blasphemy and treason - levelled against them. Such apologies were effectively petitions to the Emperor,[34] pleading for an end to the persecution of Christians who, as the defence would relate, were indicted simply for their beliefs rather than for any legal offence or political infringement.

---

[33] Breitenberg, (2003), 'To Tell the Truth'.
[34] Oscar Skarsaune, 'Justin and the Apologists', in *Routledge Companion to Early Christian Thought*, edited by DJ Bingham, (London: Routledge, 2010): 121-136.

However, whilst the biblical and classical paradigms seemed to involve a kind of performative witness in which the exemplary lifestyle represented the primary focus of an apologetic, and where the apologist sought to find shared terms of reference from which to conduct their argument, the focus within twentieth and twenty-first century apologetics has tended to be on the exposition of propositional belief as a precursor to personal conversion. As James Beilby, a leading exponent explains, 'In some cases, apologetics appropriately and naturally leads to an offer for a person to commit her life to Christ'.[35] The aim is one of offering 'the intellectual permission to believe'[36] in order to get to the point of what John Stackhouse calls 'crossing the line'[37] from non-belief to belief.

Modern apologetics has become dominated by questions such as the historicity of the resurrection[38], logical proofs of the existence of God[39], the authority of Scripture[40] and the intellectual coherence of belief.[41] Historically, however, this flies in the face of most of the trajectory of Christian apologetics which saw dialogue with surrounding culture as a necessary engagement and not simply capitulation to secular understanding. Whereas early Christian apologetics saw theology not as primarily evidential or positivist but as something that informed a way of life and articulated a whole way of being, these modern apologists have adopted what Myron Penner calls 'a kind of *apologetic positivism* … according to which Christian beliefs must be demonstrably rational to be accepted.'[42] In the best tradition of positivist science, truth,

---

[35] James K. Beilby, *Thinking about Christian Apologetics* (Downers Grove, IL: Inter-Varsity Press, 2011), 23.
[36] William Lane Craig, *On Guard: Defending your Faith with Reason and Precision* (Colorado Springs: David C. Cook, 2010), 19.
[37] John Stackhouse, *Humble Apologetics: Defending the Faith Today* (Oxford: Oxford University Press, 2002), 78.
[38] William Lane Craig, 'The Bodily Resurrection of Jesus' in *Christian Apologetics: an Anthology of Primary Sources*, edited by Khaldoun A. Sweis and Chad V. Meister (Grand Rapids: Zondervan, 2012): 362-378.
[39] Joshua Pagán, 'Defending the Existence of God', in *Making the Case for Christianity: Responding to Modern Objections*, edited by Korey D. Maas and Adam S. Francisco (St Louis: Concordia Publishing, 2014).
[40] Mark A. Pierson, 'The New Testament Gospels as Reliable History', in *Making the Case for Christianity: Responding to Modern Objections*, edited by Korey D. Maas and Adam S. Francisco (St Louis: Concordia Publishing, 2014).
[41] William Lane Craig, *Reasonable Faith: Christian Faith and Apologetics* (Third Edition), (Wheaton: Crossway Books, 2008).
[42] Myron Penner, *The End of Apologetics: Christian Witness in a Postmodern Context* (Grand Rapids: Baker Academic, 2013), 44.

argues Penner, is reduced to a 'correspondence between reality and our words by means of propositions'.[43]

In many respects, this is a strange mirror image of Enlightenment scientific positivism, in so far as it bases itself on empirical proofs and logical argument. Yet in its insistence on the primacy of propositional, evidential truth and argument, apologetics has become decontextualised, disregarding the rootedness of Christian belief in historic communities of practice or discourse and simply resting on the intellectual assent of the private individual. It is rooted in the Enlightenment paradigm of the autonomous, universal self whose capacity to discern truth is precisely dependent on their independence from external impediments or obligations: tradition, autobiography, affect, narrative, or community.[44]

Behind such a model of apologetics is also a particular view of salvation as being called out of a hostile and degenerate world. This spills over into a language, conscious or unconscious, of adversarial combat. So, for example, in the face of prevailing cultural challenges, Christians will need 'upgraded apologetic weaponry'.[45] Similarly, Tacelli and Kreeft talk about 'the battle of arguments'[46] and William Lane Craig warns that 'we've got to train our kids for war'[47]. No wonder John Stackhouse describes this as 'apologetics as martial arts'![48]

Such a dualism between 'Christ' and 'culture' also fails to see apologetics as premised on any kind of common ground – or 'bridge-building'[49] – whereby Christians and non-Christians might engage in meaningful exchange. Yet as I have been arguing, this is much closer to the pattern of the New Testament and the early Church. However, this neglect of any kind of 'cultural apologetics'[50] - or meaningful

---

[43] Penner, *The End of Apologetics*, 32.
[44] John Hughes, 'Proofs and Arguments', in *Imaginative Apologetics: Theology, Philosophy and the Catholic Tradition*, edited by Andrew Davison (London: SCM Press, 2011), 3-11; Penner, (2013), *The End of Apologetics*.
[45] John Milbank, 'An Apologia for Apologetics', in *Imaginative Apologetics: Theology, Philosophy and the Catholic Tradition*, edited by Andrew Davison (London: SCM Press, 2011), xiii.
[46] Peter Kreeft and Ronald K. Tacelli, *Pocket Handbook of Christian Apologetics* (Downers Grove, Il: Inter-Varsity Press, 2003), 139.
[47] Craig, *Reasonable Faith*, 2008, 20.
[48] Stackhouse, *Humble Apologetics*, 2002, ix.
[49] Alister McGrath, *Bridge-Building: Communicating Christianity Effectively* (Leicester: Inter-Varsity Press, 1992).
[50] John Budziszewski, *Evangelicals in the Public Square* (Grand Rapids: Baker Academic, 2006), 18-19.

engagement with the broader community via shared reference-points and common debate - represents a departure from the classical apologists' objective of making their message comprehensible to others. As John Stackhouse argues,

> Christianity ... is much more than a set of propositions to which one might or might not grant intellectual assent. It is, at its heart, a path of life, a following of Jesus Christ as disciples and as members of the worldwide Church. If apologetics consists entirely of words and truths, therefore, it will literally fail to communicate Christianity, but instead, literally distort it by shrinking it to what words and truths can portray.[51]

This is not to say that defending and commending the faith should not be carried out as an essential part of Christian witness. However, Christians today need an entirely different paradigm for their apologetics that is more appropriate to a post-secular age in which religion is both a clear and present reality in the world and a troublesome and alien phenomenon to many people.

A New Apologetics?

What kind of 'post-secular' apologetics will be fit for purpose? The task – strategic and apologetic – is essentially how to defend the enduring significance of religion, in terms of its skill at safeguarding personal well-being and its unique facility to embody significant levels of social capital within civil society when it has by and large become functionally secular.

Such a witness to faith must, in the vein of the earliest Christian apologists, step beyond the parametres of its own tradition and engage in conversations with non-Christian (religious and secular) world-views in order to demonstrate how and why Christian sources and norms are capable of shaping viable responses to the common challenges facing us all in global civil society today. The apologist must test his or her claims against competing and complementary frameworks; but having done so, they complete their task by contributing to the shaping not just of lives of believers but the common welfare of all humanity.

---
[51] Stackhouse, *Humble Apologetics*, 131.

The purpose of such apologetic dialogue is not to impose a single metaphysical dogma but to nurture constructive alliances around shared moral and political tasks.

As an act of testimony, post-secular apologetics only provides the starting-point, not the end, of dialogue, and represents a commitment on the part of the conversation partners to 'let their lives speak'. Its persuasive power rests in the way others can evaluate the extent to which Christians really do practise what they preach, to judge the worth of their words by their lives and deeds, and to encourage them to measure their own lives accordingly.[52]

Such apologetic conversation may well offer evidence that is performative rather than propositional. One example of pragmatic collaboration across different faiths and philosophies leading to this kind of constructive dialogue can be found in some of the work of two urban geographers, Justin Beaumont and Paul Cloke, in what they call 'post-secular rapprochement'. Amidst the plurality of faith groups and other agencies engaged in various forms of community partnership, especially in the city, they are discovering extraordinary 'interconnections between religious, humanist and secularist positionalities in the dynamic geographies of the city'[53]. Such collaborations are embodied in local initiatives such as food banks, youth training centres, mental health projects and asylum campaigns – enterprises that demand both a collective political and ethical response. It is out of such engaged and pragmatic dialogue, rooted in the performative praxis of faith, that post-secular apologetics can develop, as people deepen relationships built around common causes into discussions about the well-springs of their values and motivations – a sharing of what has been termed 'spiritual capital'.[54]

This is an apologetics expressed in both deed *and* word. For whilst the exercise of compassion and service does, I believe, constitute a powerful first-order theology in practice, such action still requires articulation and explanation. So the instruction to 'give an account of

---

[52] Penner, (2013), *The End of Apologetics*, 133.
[53] Justin Beaumont and Paul Cloke, 'Introduction to the Study of Faith-Based Organisations and Exclusion in European Cities', in *Faith-Based Organisations and Exclusion in European Cities*, edited by J. Beaumont and P. Cloke (London: Policy Press, 2012), 1-36, 32.
[54] Christopher Baker, 'Spiritual Capital and Economies of Grace: Redefining the Relationship between Religion and the Welfare State', *Social Policy and Society* 11.4 (2012): 565-576.

oneself' still applies, in terms of articulating the motivations behind the practices of social activism and neighbourliness. To be effective, as Max Stackhouse argues, Christian apologetics 'must show that it can form, inform and sustain the moral and spiritual architecture of a civil society so that truth, justice and mercy are more nearly approximated in the souls of persons and in the institutions of the common life.'[55] Rather than being an adversarial or confrontational process, then, the practice of apologetics becomes an invitation to dialogue. In the true spirit of public theology, it is concerned less with the fortunes of the Church than with the 'welfare of the city' (Jeremiah 29:7)[56] and with cultivating a civil, inclusive space of public debate in which all are accommodated in the name of the common good.

This is apologetics not as a weapon of conversion, but a gesture of solidarity. It respects our common places of pluralism and encounter. It is an attempt to find common cause in practices of transparency that don't seek to privilege or defend Christian supremacy, but are a means of reaching across the 'post-secular divide' to those of all faiths and none. It recognises that persons of belief must be called to account for their faith and be prepared to justify themselves; but primarily, it articulates a public vocation that is more interested in the well-being of the human family than narrow or partisan self-interest.

Apologetics and Catechesis

There remains one final question, however, which takes us into the realm of practical theology and theological education. The writer of the first letter of Peter may advise Christians to 'give an answer to the hope that is within us'; but what if we discover that we cannot find the words to articulate it? It may not only be in society at large, but crucially, within the churches that we find a deficit of religious and theological literacy. How much confidence, how much training, is the ordinary (lay) Christian given to prepare them for that apologetic task? Christians owe it to themselves as much as others to foster a

---

[55] Max Stackhouse, *God and Globalisation*, 107.
[56] Duncan B. Forrester, 'The Scope of Public Theology', *Studies in Christian Ethics* 17.2 (2004): 5-19; Andrew Bradstock, 'Seeking the welfare of the city: Public Theology as Radical Action', in *Radical Christian Voices and Practice: Essays in Honour of Christopher Rowland*, edited by Zoe Bennett and David B. Gowler (Oxford: Oxford University Press, 2012), 225-239.

greater skilfulness and articulacy in public life: to earn the right to be taken seriously, and to be willing and able to justify their moral, social and political convictions in ways that speak intelligibly into the public square. So, in the words of Marcus Borg, in order to engage effectively in Christian *apologetics* we may have to learn how to 'speak Christian' all over again.[57]

But do we need to learn to 'speak Christian' at all? If the language of faith is so off-putting, are we not better off translating everything into a general language? The answer is, I think, that we still need the nurture and foundations in the language, traditions and practices of faith. Plus, as Borg himself notes, to abandon the language of faith just because it feels anachronistic is to leave it to those who misappropriate it and render it so one-dimensional.[58]

So 'speaking Christian' into the public square may require some mediation and translation between the historical tradition and contemporary culture – but of course, that's what Christian apologists have been doing since Paul of Tarsus onwards! This kind of translation or bilingualism – of bridging one culture to another – is not the same as adopting something like Esperanto, which is an entirely new attempt at a common language. In Christian terms, Jesus is still the source of Christians' discourse about what is good, true and meaningful[59]; but the task of apologetics is then to establish some common ground on which genuine dialogue can take place. I have been suggesting that the convergent language of the common good, of a shared concern for the repair of the world represents the territory in which the best 'apologetics of presence'[60] can be practised.

The best apologists are those fully immersed in the community of faith which is where the exemplary vision of truth and goodness is nurtured; but that implies a close link between apologetics and catechesis, to enable people to learn the skills of theological reflection and argument, as well as being attuned to contemporary culture. This means, I think, that the education of the laity, and their

---

[57] Marcus Borg, *Speaking Christian: Why Christian Words Have Lost their Meaning and Power - and how they can be restored* (New York: HarperOne, 2011).
[58] Borg, (2011), *Speaking Christian*, 21-26.
[59] Borg, (2011), *Speaking Christian*, 238.
[60] Cormac Murphy-O'Connor, *'Gaudium et Spes* – The Shape of the Church: Past, Present and to Come ...' <www.thinkingfaith.org>. Accessed 9 October 2011.

'theological literacy', becomes a pressing priority for the credibility and effectiveness of Christian apologetics. But any calls for a new catechism will not address this core question of witness and apologetics if it simply requires lay Christians to learn teachings off by heart, or becoming more versed in doctrinal theology without being equipped to put that into language non-Christian people can understand, or being unable to see its relevance in terms of its practical outworkings. Nor is it resolved, I believe, by constructing programs of Christian education that are designed to 'clericalise' lay people to fulfil offices within the Church, without offering them a coherent grounding as well in the theology of their baptismal calling as the Church in the world.[61]

Conclusion

I have argued that the post-secular cannot be conceived merely as the return of Christendom or the simple 're-enchantment' of modernity. It requires us to rethink the terms on which religion is returning to the public square, both as a source of reasoning and as the motive for renewed public presence and activism. But for good reasons, such as the widespread suspicion of the very nature of those religious motives, and gulf in religious literacy, these same incursions need to be defended and justified. Increasingly, then, as practical theologians concerned for the public manifestations of religious belief and practice, we need to ask ourselves, 'How does the church 'speak Christian' into this strange new world, both fascinated and troubled by religion?'

---

[61] 'Dogmatic Constitution on the Church' (*Lumen Gentium*), in *Vatican Council II: the Conciliar and Post-Conciliar Documents*, edited by Austin Flannery (Leominster: Fowler-Wright Books, 1980), 350-432, Chapter 1.

Chapter Three

Post-Secularity and Australian Catholics

Robert Dixon

We have become accustomed to the idea that Australia is a highly secularised society, but now we also hear Australian society described as post-secular. What is meant by this term, to what extent can it be applied to Australian Catholics, and how, if at all, does it help us understand contemporary Catholicism and the challenges it faces?

In order to provide an empirical basis for these questions, the major part of this chapter sketches twelve key features of the contemporary Catholic community, all of which are informed by demographic or sociological research and which bear more or less directly on the topic under discussion. This is preceded by a short discussion of the terms 'secularisation' and 'post-secularity' and the connection between the two. There is an extensive literature on these topics and to attempt to review it in depth here would leave no room for any consideration of Australian Catholics.

The key features will be followed by two shorter sections. The first is an account of some selected articles from *The Age* newspaper that serve as an illustration that tends to persuade me that the intellectual debate in Australia remains firmly secular as opposed to post-secular. This is followed by a discussion of the disjunction that exists between the Catholic Church's traditional approach to morality and the approach taken by many contemporary Australians, including many Catholics, an approach that has arisen largely as a result of the change in Western culture over the last fifty years. Finally, I will draw all this together in a conclusion that looks at the question of whether and to what extent the term post-secularity can be applied to Australian Catholics.

Secularisation and post-secular Australia

According to the classical formulation of the secularisation thesis, there is a close and necessary link between the modernisation of society and the secularisation of the population, in that religion loses its social significance and becomes a purely private matter among a diminishing number of people.[1] However, the thesis has come under attack in recent decades and is no longer as strongly supported by sociologists as in the past,[2] leading some scholars to speak about the phenomenon of *post-secularity*.[3]

Casanova reminds us that when we speak of secularisation we need to distinguish between three different threads: the decline of religious beliefs and practices, the privatisation of religion and its disappearance from the public square, and the differentiation of secular spheres, so that rituals, services and functions in arenas such as public welfare, education and law which were once the preserve of ecclesiastical or religious authorities are transferred to civil or secular control.[4]

Habermas believes that there is still 'surprisingly robust support' for the secularisation thesis,[5] and the situation of Australia's Catholics offers a case in point. It is clear from the evidence presented in the next section that the first and third of the threads identified by Casanova are a fact of life for Catholics in Australia. The second thread—the privatisation of religion and its disappearance from the public square, is arguably not applicable, given the extent and visibility of the Catholic involvement in education, health and aged care, and social services.

The failure of the secularisation thesis, argues Habermas, lies not in its analysis of social change, but in the assumption that secularisation necessarily leads to religion's loss of influence and relevance in the political arena and culture of a society and in the way people live their lives. In reality, modern societies have to contend with what Grace

---

[1] Jurgen Habermas, 'Notes on Post-Secular Society', in *New Perspectives Quarterly*, 25 (2008): 17–29.

[2] Craig Calhoun, Mark Juergensmeyer and Jonathan VanAntwerpen, 'Introduction', in *Rethinking Secularism*, edited by Craig Calhoun, Mark Juergensmeyer and Jonathan VanAntwerpen (Oxford: Oxford University Press, 2011), 3-30.

[3] See, for example, Habermas, 'Notes on Post-Secular Society', and Elaine L Graham, *Between a Rock and a Hard Place: Public Theology in a Post-Secular Age* (London: SCM Press, 2013).

[4] José Casanova, 'Rethinking secularization: A Global Comparative Perspective, in *The Hedgehog Review*, Spring and Summer, 8/1-2 (2006): 7-22.

[5] Habermas, 'Notes on Post-Secular Society', 19.

Davie refers to as the 'persistence of religion',[6] that is, not only the reality of the ongoing existence of religious communities but also their continuing ability to actively shape social life at different levels and in a variety of forms.[7] It is this persistence of religion, and the realisation that the assumption 'to be modern meant to be secular'[8] was no longer valid, that is generally implied by the use of the term 'post-secular'.

As Beckford[9] has pointed out, the term 'post-secular' has numerous meanings, usually connected to the failure of the secularisation thesis, and sometimes suggesting a resurgence of religion. The word 'post' suggests that a post-secular society develops out of and replaces a secular one. In fact, it is more helpful to think of post-secularity as a consciousness that develops within a secular society.

The persistence of religion does not necessarily mean the flourishing of traditional forms of religion. A post-secular consciousness also involves changing perceptions of what counts as religion, a point made by Gary Bouma in Australia and Nancy Ammerman in the United States. According to Bouma:

> secular societies are not irreligious or anti-religious or lacking in spirituality... It has become extremely clear... that spirituality is not on the decline... and that religious belief and practice have moved towards the centre of many public policy issues in Australia... Rather, in secular societies religion and spirituality have seeped out of the monopolistic control of formal organisations like churches... [resulting in] vastly increased diversity of both organised religion and private spiritualties.[10]

Elsewhere, Bouma has made the comment that 'diversity is the new normal'[11] in regard to religion in Australia.

---

[6] Grace Davie, *Religion in Britain: a persistent paradox* (Oxford: Wiley Blackwell, 2015), 227.
[7] Michael Reder, 'How far can faith and reason be distinguished', in *An awareness of what is missing: faith and reason in a post-secular age*, edited by Jurgen Habermas et al. (Cambridge, UK: Polity Press, 2010), 37.
[8] Davie, *Religion in Britain*, 227.
[9] James Beckford, 'SSSR Presidential Address: Public Religions and the Postsecular: Critical Reflections', in *Journal for the Scientific Study of Religion*, 51/1 (2012): 1-19.
[10] Gary Bouma, *Australian Soul: Religion and Spirituality in the 21st Century* (Melbourne: Cambridge University Press, 2006), 5.
[11] Gary Bouma, *Being faithful in diversity* (Adelaide: ATF Press, 2011), 15.

In a similar vein, Ammerman notes that there are:

> interesting things still to learn about religion, but in a time of significant change, we cannot assume we will find religion in the predictable places or in the predictable forms. And if we do not find as much of it in those predictable places as we did before, we cannot assume that it is disappearing. Religion is not an insignificant force in the social world today, but discovering its presence and impact may require asking our questions in new ways.[12]

Three recurring elements of post-secularity in the literature, then, are diversity in religions and spiritualty, the possibility of resurgence of religion, and a willingness of secular society to engage constructively with the ongoing phenomenon of religion. To what extent are these elements in evidence in relation to Catholicism in Australia?

Key features of the contemporary Catholic community

Each of the following twelve features helps us to arrive at an answer to the question posed at the end of the previous section.[13] All of the features are described using research findings, most of which have been derived from research carried out, or in the process of being carried out, by the Pastoral Research Office of the Australian Catholic Bishops Conference. Due to the foresight of the Australian bishops establishing a social research office in 1996—one of the few bishops conferences in the world to do so—we have available a vast and regularly updated amount of sociological data on the Australian Catholic community.

---

[12] Nancy Tatom Ammerman, *Sacred Stories, Spiritual Tribes: Finding Religion in Everyday Life* (Oxford: Oxford University Press, 2013), 7-8.

[13] For a more extended account of some of these features, see Robert Dixon, 'The Changing Face of the Catholic Church in Australia: Challenges for Catholic Social Service Organisations' in *Listening, Learning and Leading: The Impact of Catholic Identity and Mission*, edited by Gabrielle McMullen and John Warhurst (Ballarat: Connor Court, 2014), 123-139. Robert Dixon and Ruth Powell, 'Vatican II: A Data-Based Analysis of its Impact on Australian Catholic Life', in *Vatican II: Reception and Implementation in the Australian Church*, edited by Neil Ormerod, Ormond Rush, David Pascoe, Clare Johnson and Joel Hodge (Mulgrave: Garratt Publishing, 2012), 292-320. Robert Dixon, 'The Science of Listening', in *The Australasian Catholic Record*, 91/3 (2014): 264-80. Robert Dixon, *The Catholic Community in Australia* (Adelaide: Openbook publishing, 2005).

1. *The Catholic population*

   According to the 2011 Australian Census, there were 5,439,268 Catholics in a total Australian population of 21,507,719.[14] This means that Catholics made up just over a quarter (25.3 per cent) of the Australian population, making them Australia's largest religious group.

   In the five years between the 2006 and 2011 Censuses, the number of Catholics increased by over 312,000, or 6.1 per cent. Catholics have continued to grow in numbers at every census, although their percentage of the Australian population has been declining slowly since the peak of 27.3 per cent in 1991. It is sometimes claimed that recent growth in the Catholic population is due almost entirely to immigration, but this is not the case. Between 2001 and 2011, for example, the overseas-born Catholic population grew by 319,577, while the Australian-born Catholic population grew by 359,975. That is, immigration and natural birth contribute about equally to the growth of the Catholic population, with the result that the percentage of the Catholic population born in Australia has remained virtually constant at around 75 per cent since at least 1991.

2. *Disidentification*

   The growth of the Catholic population might have been higher were it not for the phenomenon of disidentification. It is estimated that, across all age groups, more than 20,000 Australians cease to identify as Catholics every year, with more than half of these aged between 20 and 29.[15]

   In one sense, identification on the census form defines the limits of the Catholic community in Australia. Within that population of over 5.4 million, there is a broad spectrum of involvement and belief, from very active participants in the life of their parish, school

---

[14] For a full account of the Catholic population in the 2011 Census, see Robert Dixon and Stephen Reid, 'The Contemporary Catholic Community: A View from the 2011 Census', *Australasian Catholic Record*, 90/2 (2013). Unless otherwise noted, figures from the 2011 Australian Census in this chapter were acquired from the Australian Bureau of Statistics as part of the National Catholic Census Project 1991-2011. A comprehensive 28-page national profile of Catholics in the 2011 Census is available from http://pro.catholic.org.au/pdf/Social-Profile-of-the-Catholic-Community-in-Australia-2011-Census.pdf.

[15] Dixon and Reid, 'The Contemporary Catholic Community', 145.

or other Catholic organisation to those for whom their Catholic identity means little else than the tick on the census form.

3. *Decline in Mass attendance and ageing of attenders*

   In 2011, the number of people at Mass in Australia on a typical weekend was about 662,000, or 12.2 per cent of the total number of Catholics.[16] The 2011 National Church Life Survey (NCLS) showed that about one-third of all attenders aged 15 and over were aged between 60 and 74; people aged 80 or more made up a further eight per cent, while those aged 15 to 19 accounted for only four per cent. This age profile indicates that attendances will continue to decline, and decline quite precipitously, for some time to come. Between 1996 and 2011, despite an increase in the number of attenders who were born in non-English speaking countries, overall Mass attendances declined by about 23 per cent. This happened because the number of Australian-born attenders fell by about one-third![17]

4. *Ethnic diversity*

   One of the most striking features of the Catholic population is its ethnic diversity. Catholics are more likely to come from a non-English speaking country than Australians who are not Catholic: in 2011, 17.9 per cent of Catholics were born in a non-English speaking country, compared to 14.9 per cent of people who are not Catholic. Overall, nearly a quarter of Australia's Catholics (23.6 per cent) were born overseas. In addition, there were 124,618 Catholics of Aboriginal and Torres Strait Islander origin, accounting for 2.3 per cent of all Australia's Catholics, and 22.7 per cent of all Indigenous Australians. More than twenty non-English speaking source countries each contributed 10,000 or more people to the Australian Catholic population. The largest source of overseas-born Catholics, Italy, contributed 168,000.

---

[16] Robert Dixon, Stephen Reid and Marilyn Chee, *Mass attendance in Australia: A critical moment* (Melbourne: ACBC Pastoral Research Office, 2013). There are two main sources of data about Mass attendance. The National Counts of Attendance (2001, 2006 and 2011) collected attendance figures from all parishes and other Mass centres, as well as information about each Mass, such as the language of celebration. The National Church Life Surveys (2001, 2006 and 2011) and the 1996 Catholic Church Life Survey were conducted in a national random sample of parishes, and provide a great deal of information about Mass attenders, including their frequency of attendance, their demographic characteristics and their beliefs and practices. In 2011, a total of 47,426 completed questionnaires were received from the 217 parishes in the national sample.

[17] Dixon, Reid and Chee, *Mass attendance in Australia*, 4.

Ethnic diversity is even more pronounced among Mass attenders. In 2011, more than two-fifths (41 per cent) of the people who attend Mass in parishes were born overseas, including 33 per cent who were born in non-English speaking countries. Between 1996 and 2011, the attendance rate of Australian-born Catholics fell from about 17 per cent to ten per cent, while the attendance rate of Catholics born in non-English speaking countries remained reasonably steady at around 23 per cent.

5. *Diversity of beliefs among Mass attenders*

The 2011 NCLS included questions about four key beliefs of the Catholic Church: the Trinitarian nature of God, the Virgin Birth, Transubstantiation and the bodily Resurrection of Christ.[18]

By and large, Mass-going Catholics display a high degree of orthodoxy, as indicated by the high levels of acceptance of these four key Catholic doctrines by respondents in the 2011 NCLS. Nine in ten (90 per cent) said they believe that the consecrated bread and wine at Mass become the sacred Body and Blood of Christ, 84 per cent selected a Trinitarian statement as best expressing their understanding of God, 75 per cent expressed belief in the virginal conception of Jesus, and 71 per cent assented to the statement that 'Christ was raised by God's power from death to life—really, bodily, physically'. This high level of orthodoxy is not unexpected among Mass-attending Catholics; what might be considered surprising is that the level of orthodoxy is not even higher. It is older attenders and attenders born in non-Western countries, particularly India, Sri Lanka and the Philippines, who tend to hold more orthodox views compared to attenders who were born in Australia and younger attenders, although the differences by age were only very moderate for each of the beliefs in question.

6. *Declining numbers and ageing of Australian-born clergy & increasing numbers of overseas-born clergy*

The number of priests in Australia has been gradually declining since the late 1960s. In 1967, for example, there were 2,389

---

[18] For a full discussion of these questions, see Robert Dixon, 'What Do Mass Attenders Believe? Contemporary Cultural Change and the Acceptance of Key Catholic Beliefs and Moral Teachings by Australian Mass Attenders', in *Australasian Catholic Record*, 90/4 (2013): 439–58.

diocesan priests and 1,397 religious order priests in Australia.[19] By 2016, those numbers had fallen to 1,948 and 1,003 respectively,[20] and their average age has also most likely increased; although there is no comprehensive age data available, the fact that the current *Official Directory* lists 491 diocesan priests as retired suggests an ageing population. The decline has been offset to a large extent by recruiting priests and seminarians from overseas; in 2014, there were 150 priests born in India working in Australia's dioceses. These include both diocesan priests and members of religious orders who have been recruited, usually through agreements between the diocesan bishop and the order in India, to work in a particular Australian diocese.[21] The corresponding numbers for the other major source countries were Vietnam (89), the Philippines (75), Ireland (68), Nigeria (37), Malta (27) and Poland (27).[22] The patterns of arrival in Australia differ markedly between these birthplace groups. While the vast majority of the priests from India have come to Australia in recent years, most of the Irish-born priests have been in Australia for many years, and many of the priests born in Vietnam actually grew up in Australia, while others came here to do their seminary training and then remained in Australia after ordination.

7. *Disappearance of religious sisters and brothers from Church life*

If the decline in the number of clergy has been relatively modest, the same cannot be said for the decline in the number of religious sisters and brothers. In 1967, there were 13,720 religious sisters and 2,234 religious brothers.[23] By 2016, those numbers were 4,394 and 680 respectively.[24] A 2009 study[25] of Catholic religious in

---

[19] *The Official Year Book of the Catholic Church of Australia, New Zealand and Oceania 1967-1968* (Sydney: EJ Dwyer).
[20] *The Official Directory of the Catholic Church in Australia July 2016–June 2017* (Belmont, Vic: National Council of Priests, 2016), 795.
[21] The number does not include Indian-born priests who belong to religious orders with organisational structures in Australia, such as the Jesuits.
[22] These preliminary figures are based on diocesan returns to a survey conducted by the ACBC Pastoral Research Office in August 2014..
[23] *The Official Year Book of the Catholic Church of Australia, New Zealand and Oceania 1967-1968* (Sydney: EJ Dwyer).
[24] *The Official Directory of the Catholic Church in Australia July 2016–June 2017* (Belmont, Vic: National Council of Priests, 2016), 796.
[25] Stephen Reid, Robert Dixon and Noel Connolly, *See I am Doing a New Thing:*

Australia found that the median age of religious sisters was 74, and that there were only 36 religious brothers under the age of 50. This decline has had an enormous impact on Catholicism in Australia. Students attending Catholic schools in the 1950s would certainly have been taught by a religious sister, brother or priest. In the 1960s, religious still made up most of the teaching staff and occupied almost all the senior leadership positions, but students in most Catholic schools today would rarely if ever encounter a religious sister or brother. A similar disappearance from view has happened in most other Catholic institutions such as hospitals. Whereas for earlier generations of Catholics, religious sisters and, to a lesser extent, brothers, were a very obvious part of Catholic life, for today's Catholics religious have become almost invisible.

8. *Changing views and practices regarding marriage and sexuality*

Catholics, even Mass attending Catholics, vary a great deal in their views and practices about a range of issues to do with marriage and sexuality, and do not always agree with or act according to the Church's teaching.

Results of the 2011 NCLS show that considerable proportions of Mass attenders hold views that differ from the Church's teaching with regard to pre-marital sex, artificial contraception, and the exclusion from communion of people who have divorced and remarried without an annulment of their previous marriage. For example, fewer than half (42 per cent) of Mass attenders accept the Church's teaching that pre-marital sex is always wrong,[26] and 40 per cent do not accept the practice whereby divorced Catholics who have remarried without an annulment of their previous marriage are refused Communion (a further 16 per cent say they don't know whether they accept it or not).[27] Among Mass attenders for whom the question is applicable, there is a big difference between the percentages of those who say they use artificial means of birth control and those who use only natural family planning methods—49 per cent compared to six per cent.[28]

---

[26] Dixon, 'The Changing Face of the Catholic Church in Australia', 133.
[27] Dixon, 'The Science of Listening', 270.
[28] Unpublished figures from the 2011 National Church Life Survey.

Also in the 2011 NCLS, Mass attenders were asked whether same-sex couples should be able to marry, and whether same-sex couples should be able to register their relationships as civil unions. While Mass attenders were strongly opposed to same sex marriage (64 per cent disagree, 16 per cent agree, with 19 per cent undecided or unsure), the percentage disagreeing with civil unions was only marginally higher than the percentage agreeing that they should be allowed (42 per cent compared to 39 per cent, and again with 19 per cent undecided). Younger attenders, the highly educated, newcomers and infrequent attenders were the most likely to support same-sex marriage and civil unions.[29] In contrast, Catholics in general (as distinct from Mass attenders) were more nearly like the general population in their attitudes to same sex marriage. A June 2014 survey commissioned by Australian Marriage Equality found that 72 per cent of Australians, and 67 per cent of those who identified as Catholic, said they would support allowing same-sex couples to marry.[30]

In 1967, 89.3 per cent of marriages in Australia were performed by ministers of religion, and 10.7 per cent by civil celebrants. By 2012, the corresponding figures were 28.1 per cent and 71.9 per cent respectively.[31] There are no figures available for the percentage of marriages performed by civil celebrants where either or both partners are Catholics, but the number of marriages celebrated according to the rites of the Church fell from 22,139 in 1993 to 11,688 in 2012, a drop of 47 per cent in just 19 years.[32]

9. *Decline of traditional religious practices*

Another feature of Catholic life where we have seen change is in the decline of traditional religious practice. Thanks to a 1974 survey conducted by anthropologist and Columban priest, the late Cyril Hally, we are able to make a direct comparison between 1974

---

[29] Nicole Hancock, Miriam Pepper and Ruth Powell, *Attitudes to same-sex marriage and civil unions*, NCLS Research Fact Sheet 14015 (Adelaide: Mirrabooka Press, 2014).

[30] The question asked by market research company Crosby Textor was 'Based on what you know at this point in time, would you support or oppose allowing same-sex couples to marry in Australia?' Crosby Textor, 'Same-Sex Marriage Research 2014: Summary Results', 27 June 2014. <http://www.crosbytextor.com/news/crosby-textor-same-sex-marriage-research-2014>. Accessed 16 April 2016.

[31] Australian Institute of Family Studies, 'Marriage in Australia Source Data', <https://aifs.gov.au/facts-and-figures/marriage-australia/marriage-australia-source-data#celebrants.> Accessed 1 June 2016.

[32] Secretaria Status, *Statistical Yearbook of the Church 1993* (Vatican City: Libreria Editrice Vaticana, 1995); Secretaria Status, *Statistical Yearbook of the Church 2012* (Vatican City: Libreria Editrice Vaticana, 2014). See also Dixon, *The Catholic Community in Australia*, 113-5.

and 2011 about two practices of Mass attenders in the Diocese of Ballarat. In 1974, 31 per cent of Mass attenders in Ballarat Diocese said they recited the Rosary frequently (at least several times per week) and half (49 per cent) reported that they went to confession at least monthly.[33] By 2011, these figures for the diocese had fallen to eighteen per cent and seven per cent respectively.[34]

Across Australia, the practice of individual confession has declined steeply: in 2011, more than half (54 per cent) of Mass attenders said they had not been to the First Rite of Reconciliation in the previous twelve months, and 66 per cent had not been to a celebration of the Second Rite. More than three-fifths of Mass attenders either do not go to confession at all these days (30 per cent) or else they go less often than they used to five years ago (32 per cent).[35]

10. *Disconnection from the lives of ordinary Catholics*

Research published in 2007[36] found that the single most important reason mature-age, long-term Mass attenders gave for ceasing to attend was that they experienced a disconnection between what the Church saw as important and what they thought was important for their lives. They believed that the Church is out of touch with contemporary society and is not relevant to their lives. They saw this lack of connection as arising out of both their own changing personal circumstances and a failure of the Church to adapt to changes in Australian society and culture.

Most participants in the research spoke about the vital importance for them of nurturing a continuing spiritual dimension in their lives. For some, that spiritual dimension had a strong connection to the Catholic tradition, while for others their current spirituality had little or no connection with the Christian faith or any organised form of religion.

---

[33] Cyril Hally, *Report on a Survey of the Religious Attitudes of the People of the Diocese of Ballarat* (Ballarat: Diocese of Ballarat, 1975).
[34] Unpublished figures from the 2011 National Church Life Survey.
[35] Dixon, 'The Science of Listening', 271.
[36] Robert Dixon, Sharon Bond, Kath Engebretson, Richard Rymarz, Bryan Cussen and Katherine Wright, *Catholics who have stopped attending Mass: Final report* (Melbourne: Australian Catholic Bishops Conference, 2007).

11. Disillusionment with Church authorities over clergy sexual abuse

One variant of the 2011 NCLS answered by a subsample of Mass attenders included a set of questions about their attitude to the clergy sexual abuse crisis. Half of all attenders (49 per cent) expressed agreement with the statement that 'the cases of sexual abuse by priests and religious have damaged my confidence in Church authorities', and 54 per cent agreed that the response of Church authorities had been inadequate and showed a complete failure of responsibility. However, 56 per cent agreed that the Church now seemed to be taking appropriate steps to meet its responsibilities. In a sign that attenders distinguish between the failure of the institution and the crimes of individual offenders, on the one hand, and the majority of priests and religious on the other, only 26 per cent said that their respect for priests and religious had declined as a result of the crisis. Nevertheless, their generally high degree of orthodoxy, mentioned earlier, does not prevent them from being critical of the institution and its leaders.

We do not know what impact, if any, the crisis has had on Mass attendance. The decline in attendance between the national counts of 2006 and 2011 was consistent with the declines of the previous 25 years or so; there did not appear to be any acceleration of decline that could be attributed to the sex abuse crisis. This will be something to keep an eye on when the national attendance figures for 2016 become available.

12. Catholics in Australian society

It is easy enough to fall into the trap of talking about Catholics and Australian society, as though they were distinct entities. In fact, Catholics are a large part of Australian society. It is not possible to separate them, as one might possibly do with the members of a small and separatist sect. A few figures will suffice to make the point here. At the time of the 2011 Census, Catholic schools educated 22 per cent of Australia's primary and secondary students, and 27.5 per cent of those were not Catholics. A research project currently being conducted by the Pastoral Research Office on behalf of the Australian Catholic Council for Employment

Relations (ACCER) aims to count the number of people employed by Catholic organisations throughout Australia—parishes, schools, diocesan agencies, hospitals, aged care facilities, social service agencies and so on. An early estimate is that the number will turn out to be around 220,000, making the Church and its associated institutions one of the largest employers in the nation. Yet the relationship between Church, employee and client is ambiguous, unclear and complex. The Church might see these organisations as instruments of education, charity, justice and evangelisation, but not all employees—and not even all the Catholics among them—see it that way, and not all are happy to be considered employees of the Church.[37] This situation is behind the urgent necessity for Catholic bodies to work on issues to do with their identity and mission.

The picture of Australian Catholicism that emerges from this brief review is that despite an increasing Catholic population, there are numerous signs of decline within the Church: disidentification, falling Mass attendances, declines in devotional practices, diversification of beliefs and of moral attitudes and behaviours, particularly in relation to sexuality and marriage, accompanied by declining numbers and increasing ethnic diversity among the clergy and a virtual disappearance of religious sisters and brothers from the active life of the Church. Many Catholics report feeling a sense of disconnection from the Church and have been dismayed by the clergy sexual abuse crisis and the perceived failure of Church leaders to deal appropriately with the situation. However, the very size of the Catholic population and of the Church's enterprises in education, health care and other sectors means that there is a continuous and largely productive interaction between the Church and the rest of Australian society.

---

[37] Since this paper was written, a report on this study has been published and is available at https://www.accer.asn.au/. See Robert Dixon, Jane McMahon, Stephen Reid, George Keryk and Annemarie Atapattu, *Our Work Matters: Catholic Church employers and employees in Australia*, (Fitzroy, Australian Catholic Bishops Conference, 2017). I once mentioned the ACCER project to an employee at ACU, and mentioned that she would therefore be counted as part of the project. Her response was a vehement 'I don't work for the Catholic Church—I work for a publicly funded university'.

The defence of secularity

In my experience, the concept of post-secularity, the idea that modern societies have to contend with the reality of the ongoing existence of religion and its continuing ability to actively shape society, is keenly contested in Australian intellectual life. There is no doubt that religion remains prominent in Australian society. It is in the newspapers every day—the sex abuse crisis in the Catholic Church, Islamic State terrorism and opposition to the erection of a new mosque in Bendigo are just some examples—and it may well be true that spirituality and religion, broadly conceived, are flourishing in the lives of ordinary Australians. But in intellectual discourse, religion is very often portrayed in an unfavourable light, and its right to contribute to public debates is disputed and its contribution disparaged. As Canadian philosopher Charles Taylor notes, the Christian worldview is judged to be a dangerous illusion and Christian faith is regarded as something that needs to be overcome and set firmly in the past if humanism is to flourish.[38]

As evidence of this reluctance to engage with religion, and particularly with Christianity, let me briefly draw attention to several articles that have appeared in the pages of Melbourne's *The Age* newspaper in the last year or so. For example, on Christmas Eve in 2015, *The Age* published an article by Leslie Cannold, whose past appointments include providing research expertise to the Department of Health's Human Research Ethics Committee,[39] in which she proposed the idea that 'what may be required during our nearly 90 years on earth is not one romantic partnership, but three' in order to 'match the three distinct stages of contemporary life'.[40] In an article published in *The Age* in February 2016, sex therapist Matty Silver wrote that three people of any sex having sex together can be 'a fun diversion; another option of making . . . sex lives more interesting . . . Having a threesome can be a relationship rejuvenator if you have a strong bond

---

[38] Charles Taylor, *A Catholic Modernity. Charles Taylor's Marianist Award Lecture*, edited by James L Heft SM (New York: Oxford University Press, 1999), 15.
[39] Leslie Cannold, 'About', <http://cannold.com/about>. Accessed 2 April 2016.
[40] Leslie Cannold, 'Wedded bliss, until the next stage do us part', <http://www.theage.com.au/comment/marriage-can-be-heaven-or-hell-and-if-yours-is-making-you-miserable-get-out-20151222-gltqwu.html>, Accessed 24 December 2015.

and want to explore together. It can be really positive experience.'[41] It is not just Christian moral values and practices that are challenged in *The Age*. In some ways the very foundations of Christianity are picked apart, piece by piece. On Good Friday this year (2016), The Age carried an opinion piece by Rationalist Society President and Sex Party candidate, Meredith Doig, under the title 'Religion's tax break is a cross we shouldn't have to bear' in which she argued against tax exemptions for religious organisations.[42] In itself, raising questions about tax exemptions for religious organisations is valid and the questions ought to be debated. But in the course of her article she asked 'Is there anything in the definition of religion that makes it intrinsically charitable?' Perhaps not in the Australian High Court's definition of religion that she makes use of, but to anyone who knows anything at all about Christianity its intrinsic emphasis on charity is obvious. Doig uses a secular, legal definition about religion in general to call into question the very essence of one particular religion.

It must be said that not all writing about Christianity in *The Age* is negative.[43] In fact, The Age was one of the last of the major newspapers to have a religion editor, the last incumbent (for twelve years), being Barney Zwartz, a practising Christian and, since his retirement from *The Age*, a Senior Fellow of the Centre for Public Christianity. As Zwartz observed in a thoughtful article in December 2015,[44] forgiveness is another contested Christian virtue. In the article, he presents the Christian view that 'forgiveness is a moral imperative, even though they [Christians] may fall short in that command as they do in others. But for believer and non-believer alike, forgiveness carries the psychological benefit of liberating the victim from negative

---

[41] Matty Silver, 'How to Have a Threesome', <http://www.theage.com.au/lifestyle/life/how-to-have-a-threesome-20160201-gmj299.html>. Accessed 2 April 2016.

[42] Meredith Doig, 'Religion's tax break is a cross we shouldn't have to bear', <http://www.theage.com.au/comment/easter-is-a-good-time-to-revisit-taxexempt-status-of-religious-organisations-20160323-gnpzjj.html>. Accessed 2 April 2016.

[43] *The Age* also publishes the occasional article defending the Christian viewpoint. Barney Zwartz himself can be relied upon to present a Christian view and, on Easter Sunday 2016, *The Age* published an article by Economics Editor Ross Gittins, another Fellow of the Centre for Public Christianity, on the Christian foundations of economics, an article for which he was mercilessly chastised in the 122 comments which were posted under the online version of the article. See Ross Gittins, 'Economy Rests on Christian Foundations', <http://www.theage.com.au/business/the-economy/economy-rests-on-christian-foundations-20160324-gnq5io>. Accessed 2 April 2016.

[44] Barney Zwartz, 'Can we truly forgive? Is the Christian demand relevant today?'<http://www.theage.com.au/national/can-we-truly-forgive-is-the-christian-demand-relevant-today-20151215-glolqk>. Accessed 2 April 2016.

emotions.' Other contemporary voices see it differently. Zwartz quotes author Robert Dessaix and professor of psychiatry at Melbourne University, Louise Newman, who both question, from different perspectives, the Christian notion of forgiveness. Dessaix believes that forgiveness works only for devout believers because, in his view, they are confident that God will eventually fix the account. Newman says she wants to help people accept what has happened so they can live with it, but not to forgive the perpetrators 'because they should not be forgiven'.

In aggregate, it appears that the majority view of opinion writers in *The Age* is that the influence of organised religion is intolerable in a secular and progressive society. And, in fact, Age columnist Clementine Ford argued exactly that in another 2015 article.[45] Even the good that Christianity has done over the centuries in terms of helping to lay the moral foundations of Western civilisation is now portrayed as not only out of date but as oppressive, discriminatory and abusive, in other words, as a thoroughgoing evil influence in society. I am sure it is no accident that these articles tend to appear in the newspaper around major Christian feasts like Easter and Christmas. It appears to me that dominant viewpoint of *The Age* remains firmly secularist, as opposed to post-secularist, especially towards the Catholic Church, in that there is little evidence to be found its pages of any post-secular acceptance of a resurgence in religion or a positive attempt to engage with its place in Australian society

A culture of rights

Before I conclude, I want to make an observation about a disjunction in approaches to moral questions between the Catholic Church and many Australians, including especially young, intelligent and morally thoughtful Catholics, a disjunction that arose as a result of the process of secularisation. According to Taylor, the cultural shift that began in Western societies such as Australia in the 1960s led to people understanding life to mean 'that each one of us has his/her own way

---

[45] Clementine Ford, 'Want equality for all? Then spurn organised religion', <http://www.theage.com.au/comment/want-equality-for-all-then-spurn-organised-religion-20150501-1mxmtg.html>. Accessed 2 April 2016.

of realizing our humanity, and that it is important to find and live out one's own, as against surrendering to conformity with a model imposed on us from outside, by society, or the previous generation, or religious or political authority'.[46] This in turn led to a widespread emphasis on the importance of immediate experience, self-exploration and self-determination,[47] and the development of a morality based on individual rights which has become a defining feature of contemporary Australian society. It has been apparent to me that a major cause of the clash between the Church's moral teachings and the moral positions adopted by a large proportion of contemporary Australians, Catholics included, lies in the disjunction between this rights-based morality and the natural law approach favoured by the Church.[48]

The two approaches overlap to a large extent. Both recognise the importance of the person and aim to protect human dignity, and they often arrive at the same conclusions: from both perspectives, for example, murder, rape and theft are wrong. It is because of the high degree of overlap, and the tendency we all have to see the world without being aware of our underlying assumptions, that the differences inherent in the two approaches are often not noticed.

The two approaches, however, can and do come into conflict. A very prominent issue where conflict is evident at the moment is in relation to the question of same-sex marriage. From the point of view of Catholic teaching, same-sex marriage involves a serious violation of the natural law, which ties together the relational and procreative dimensions of human sexuality. In this view, sexual activity between members of the same sex is always objectively evil. However, when looked at from the perspective of individual rights, as most Australians now appear to do, gay sex is fine if that is how two people freely choose to express their love for each other, and they have as much right as heterosexual couples to have their unions recognised

---

[46] CharlesTaylor, *A Secular Age* (Cambridge, MA: Bellknap Press, 2007), 475.
[47] Robert Dixon, What Do Mass Attenders Believe? Contemporary Cultural Change and the Acceptance of Key Catholic Beliefs and Moral Teachings by Australian Mass Attenders, *The Australasian Catholic Record*, 90/4 (2013), 440.
[48] For an extended account of this disjunction, see Ethna Regan, 'Natural Law as Conjunctive and Disjunctive: Through the Lens of Hiberno-Christendom', in *Church and People: Disjunctions in a Secular Age*, edited by Charles Taylor, José Casanova and George F. McLean (Washington DC: The Council for Research in Values and Philosophy, 2012).

by civil authorities. For the Church, evil is the deliberate violation of the natural law; for contemporary Australians, especially younger Australians, evil is the deliberate prevention of people from exercising their rights. This is a distinction that Catholic Church leaders have, in general, so far failed to grasp. From their perspective, they think that people are misinformed, manipulated by evil forces, or actively hostile to traditional authority when they support same-sex marriage and oppose the Church's teaching. They have failed to see that in the eyes of so many people, it is the Church that is actually perpetrating evil by impeding the free exercise of individual rights. No wonder Church leaders are bewildered by the level of hostility they provoke.

This disjunction is not going to be quickly or easily overcome. Both approaches tend to rigidity in different ways: natural law for its perceived tendency to lack compassion in the rigorous application of the general law (although Pope Francis has worked towards overcoming this in *Amoris Laetitia*[49]). In the case of rights, the rigidity lies in an ever-expanding and sometimes trivial catalogue of what constitutes fundamental rights, coupled with variation by region, class and ethnicity as to what is recognised as a right. Nevertheless, as Taylor points out,[50] it is only through the emergence of a rights-based morality that Catholicism came to accept full equality of rights for all people, including atheists, people of other religions, and those who are seen as violating the Christian moral code,[51] that is, that Catholicism became truly catholic.

It is very important for the Church to recognise this disjunction if it is to understand why young people, especially, see the Church as reactionary, out-of-date, abusive, anachronistic and even evil. Attempts to evangelise people who see the world this way will not be successful if the approach is simply to tell them that they are wrong.

---

[49] Pope Francis, *Amoris Laetitia* (2016), n. 308.
[50] Taylor, *A Catholic Modernity*, 17.
[51] Taylor, *A Catholic Modernity*, 17.

Conclusion

The Catholic people and Catholic institutions are interwoven with Australian society, and cannot help but be affected by the secular nature of that society and any post-secular trends that emerge from within it. Indeed, they also influence and in some cases help to initiate those trends.

Let us now return to the questions with which I began this chapter: to what extent can the term 'post-secular' be applied to Australian Catholics, and how does it help us understand contemporary Catholicism and the challenges it faces? We can look at these questions in terms of the three elements of post-secularity identified earlier: resurgence of religion, a willingness of secular society to engage constructively with the ongoing phenomenon of religion, and diversity in religions and spiritualty.

Despite strenuous efforts and isolated successful initiatives, there is little evidence of any resurgence of religion among Australian Catholics. The overall picture that emerges from the sketches above is one of decline: in Mass attendance, devotional practices, numbers of priests and religious, and so on. Furthermore, the age and ethnic profiles of the most active Catholics suggests that the decline will continue for some considerable time, culminating in a Church in which Catholics from non-English speaking countries will predominate, while second and subsequent generations of Australians will largely be absent.

At the institutional level, as I have pointed out elsewhere[52], three of the four major sectors of the Church in Australia—Catholic education, Catholic health and aged care, and Catholic social services—are flourishing. However, the parish sector is struggling and close to collapse in some places. This is, of course, largely because it is the parishes that are the first to suffer from the declines in participation and practice noted earlier, and because this decline creates financial pressures as well. It is also the parishes that have most keenly felt the decline in the number of priests and the impact of the practice in some dioceses of replacing them whenever possible with recently arrived priests from overseas, many of whom lack training or suitability for work in an Australian context.

---

[52] Dixon, 'The Science of Listening', 278-80.

How willing is Australia's secular society to engage with Catholicism? The Catholic Church as an institution is widely regarded in a very negative light, largely as a result of its own failings in handling the clergy sexual abuse crisis, even though its schools, hospitals and social services are generally held in high esteem. But the sex abuse crisis has been a confirmation of rather than a trigger for much of the negative discourse directed at the Church. We have seen a hardening of attitudes towards the Church, and a strengthening of the view that the Church has no right to express its views in the public square, or even in its own schools, as the recent unsuccessful complaint against the Archdiocese of Hobart shows.[53]

In another sense, though, the Catholic Church is a respected participant in Australian society, especially in respect of its schools, hospitals and social welfare organisations. In one sense, it is too big not to engage with. It is what Casanova calls a 'public religion'.[54]

Diversity is a prominent characteristic of Australian Catholicism, most obviously in demographic and especially ethnic terms, but also in terms of attendance, belief, devotional practices and moral attitudes. Diversification in these things results in some attenders ceasing to attend Mass, and some people ceasing to identify as Catholics, as their search for, or discovery of, new religious or spiritual meaning leads them away from Catholicism towards other religions or none.

When we speak of post-secularity and Australian Catholics, this is what we need to keep in mind—the continuing public prominence of the Church, in both the positive sense of its contribution to Australian society, and in a negative sense, epitomised in its institutional failure in regard to clergy sexual abuse, and the fact that ordinary Australian Catholics are likely to be increasingly diverse in their religious practices, beliefs, spiritualties and attitudes towards the institutional Church. But diversity in Catholicism is not something to be feared or reined in; Charles Taylor reminds us that it is intrinsic to the notion of 'catholic'; it is part of the way in which we are made in the image of God.[55]

---

[53] Archdiocese of Hobart, 'Anti-discrimination complaint: No case to answer', https://www.facebook.com/ArchdioceseofHobart/, Accessed 1 June 2016.
[54] José Casanova, Public religions in the modern world (Chicago: University of Chicago Press, 1994).
[55] Taylor, *A Catholic Modernity*, 15.

Chapter Four

Towards a Practical Political Theology: A Provisional Typology of Public Faith in a Post-Secular Age

Andrew Cameron

Even after two millennia of churches relating to political cultures that surround them, we're still not entirely clear what to do.

This statement is not offered in despair, or to counsel other-worldly withdrawal. 'What to do' in relation to the political cultures that surround us—a question of Christian political ethics—can never be straightforwardly settled in advance by some theory of church and state. All ethical deliberation and action upholds enduring norms, but does so within the flux of a thousand variables and considerations that can only be known by *those* actors in *this* context in *that* place.

In this chapter, I will appropriate some core insights in current Christian theological ethics to help us navigate the shoals and currents of your or my particular local polity. I seek for a way to think about politics that is less committed to grand theory and disputes about it, and more able to move practically into the world—albeit well-informed by political theology, by our faith gone public, and by canny awareness of the shifting canons in our 'secular' (or increasingly 'post-secular') culture.

I will construct a 'typology' of sorts, framed by two basic axes of response. One axis concerns the kinds of moral response we take on this or that issue. Then, the ways we think of our church relating to our local political culture are plotted on the other axis. It turns out that we might locate ourselves differently on each axis depending on the specific political question before us.

I hope to show that we do not, and probably cannot, make global decisions about what theory to use for every political question; but that we can and do have the Christian wit and wisdom to consider creatively some candidate approaches to this or that political issue or question. This style of thinking can also help to defuse disputes among Christians when they differ in approach, for we begin to see what drives our Christian 'opponent'. It may be that they differ in their initial moral reasoning about the matter; it may be that they are working to a different account of their relation to their local political culture; or even (*contra* what I espouse) that they apply a global meta-theory of that relation to every political question, or even to every political culture.

The eighteenth-century thinker Johann Georg Hamann might not seem an obvious starting-point for a discussion of the public expressions of faith. But he alerts us to what goes on beneath visibility in various expressions of public theology. Hamann was a friend and contemporary of Immanuel Kant, and eventually his sworn opponent. He was very aware of the impact of our affections upon our evaluative judgments, and opposed the universalising, cognitivist conceits of German idealism long before Kantianism dominated Western conceptions of ethics.

He urges us to 'observe for yourselves the manifestations of the passions everywhere in human society; as everything, no matter how remote, strikes the mind's affect in a particular way; as every single sensation extends over the compass of all external objects.'[1] So it is to be a human. We are grounded in our immediate responses to what surrounds us. We attach with vigour to what seems to us to matter. Hamann would have been unsurprised by the raw emotivism of our internet, with its memes and hotspots.

But Hamann goes on to notice the way we then 'appropriate universal cases by a personal application, and blow up every parochial situation into a public spectacle of heaven and earth. Every individual truth grows into the foundation of a plan . . . and a plan more ample

---

[1] Johann Georg Hamann, 'Aesthetica in Nuce', in *Johann Georg Hamann's Relational Metacriticism*, translated by Gwen Griffith Dickson (Berlin; New York: Walter de Gruyter, 1995), 422–423.

than the hemisphere contains the tip of a point-of-view. In brief, the perfection of projects, the strength of their exposition; the conception and birth of new ideas and new expressions; the work and rest of the wise, their consolation and disgust in it, lie in the fruitful womb of the passions buried before our senses.'[2]

His (notoriously) dense and pregnant point is to unmask how given we are to totalising our passions. Our plans, projects, rhetoric, and the parameters of our daily work all spring from what matters to us; and arise, ultimately, from these moments of passionate attachment to what lies before our senses. That our plan becomes 'more ample than the hemisphere contains the tip of a point-of-view' uses a marvellous metaphor to describe how prone we are to over-extend our perceptions. Our single point of view on the globe can only go to the horizon; but our moments of passionate attachment extend beyond the senses into grand visions that tip over the horizon into audaciously global causes, far beyond perception.

This intriguing passage takes very seriously the intuitions of our affections, particularly at a time when Kant's dismissal of 'passion' was about to take the stage in philosophical ethics and later, in Rawlsian political theory. Our intuitions may not always prove right. But Hamann has noticed that we cannot proceed as if we don't begin there. In the language of Augustine, we are constituted, in part, by what we love.[3]

Hamann sheds light on the plethora of advocacy positions, and the largeness of each advocate's plan, in Australian public life in general and in public theology in particular. Australian political scientist Rodney Smith has calculated that during our 2007 Federal Election, church and parachurch organisations advocated different positions and commended different parties on at least 47 distinct issues,[4] so that 'pluralism rather than ideological consensus best defines the approach of the churches as a whole in 2007'.[5]

---

[2] Hamann, (1995), 'Aesthetica', 423.
[3] 'In our present state, we believe that we possess these three things—being, knowledge and love—not on the testimony of others, but because we ourselves are aware of their presence, and because we discern them with our most truthful inner vision.' Augustine, *The City of God Against the Pagans*, translated by R.W. Dyson (Cambridge: Cambridge University Press, 1998), 488 (XI.28).
[4] Rodney Smith, 'How Would Jesus Vote? The Churches and the Election of the Rudd Government', *Australian Journal of Political Science* 44/4 (2009): 622.
[5] Smith, (2009), 'How would Jesus Vote?', 632.

Marcus Smith and Peter Marden observe that:

> The degree to which an individual's perception of the world and humanity's place in it are shaped by religion can have profound implications for politics. But to distinguish a relationship in any concrete sense is fraught with problems owing to the lack of conceptual clarity as to what exactly defines the boundaries of the political and religious.
>
> This is further complicated by the complex mix of beliefs in the divine and metaphysical, not all of which recognise a deity as the supreme manifestation of authority and order.[6]

In terms of actual political effectiveness, John Warhurst comments that such a variety of voices can only amount to cottage-level politicking, which is naïve and ineffective in modern party politics.[7] But whatever our aspiration might be for a more united political effectiveness, we also do well to map the current cacophony and its reasons. For if Hamann is right, each plan and movement and project has begun in the fruitful womb of the passions of each pundit and their party. I want at least to try to map this complexity a little.

I'll begin, first, with the thought that from the polity of the church erupts ways of being social that can affect other local polities. But *how* that occurs is far from clear or settled. After a small interlude on typology, I'll go on to propose a two-axis typology of some modes of engagement that people of faith seem to deploy in their engagements with other polities.

One axis consists of four primal moral postures that people adopt toward others on various issues. I call these 'cooperation', 'subversion', 'exposure' and 'separation'. They represent four kinds of relationship with others arising from our basic moral commitments. None of these postures is necessarily better than another, and discernment entails intentionality about which posture is required in any new situation.

---

[6] Marcus Smith and Peter Marden, 'Capturing the Religious Spirit: A Challenge for the Secular State', *Journal of Church and State*, 55/1 (2013): 31.
[7] John Warhurst, 'Politics, Religion and Election Issues', talk presented to *Social Policy Connections*, Wednesday 4 August 2011, at <http://www.socialpolicyconnections.com.au/podcasts/Politics%20Religion%20Election%20Issues.mp3>. Accessed 27 November 2015.

The other axis includes four reactions to government that Christians habitually deploy. I'll call these 'translation', 'demarcation', 'embodiment' and 'restoration'. Each discloses some deeper predisposition on the legitimacy of government.

These types of reaction express affectionate responses by Christian political citizens toward their local polities. They defy analysis according to the logic of any one grand theory. They may also liberate our political imaginations if we attend to them.

The Polity of the Church

According to the early Christian scriptures, 'God placed all things under his feet and appointed him to be head over everything for the church, which is his body, the fullness of him who fills everything in every way' (Ephesians 1:22–23). Therefore 'all rule and authority, power and dominion, and every title that can be given' (v. 21) are subservient to the Church's Lord. On this reasoning, it follows that human social orderings offer no pattern for proper sociality in the church. As his 'body', the church takes its form from him alone.

Of course, it does not always seem so. Actual churches clubbishly reflect local cultures, harbour sins and reify cultural distortions. The early twentieth-century Congregationalist theologian P. T. Forsyth knew as much. But even so, he hoped in what he called the gospel's 'creative, self-organising, and self-recuperative power',[8] and in that light, considered the relationship of a church so patterned to the democracy of his time. As World War 1 escalates, he writes that 'we have rediscovered Satan. We are in the kind of world-crisis in which creeds are reborn for history... We shall therefore need, as none living have ever before felt the need, a religion which shows that it possesses the innate power of the Holy to deal with the wild beast which a high and Christless civilisation shows itself to be'[9]—as pertinent in a world of predator drones and industrialised sex.

If the gospel has such a power to create, organise and recuperate, then from it will spring the church's own unique 'polity', with affections

---

[8] Peter Taylor Forsyth, *Lectures on the Church and the Sacraments* (London: Longmans Green & Co, 1917), 42.
[9] Forsyth, *Church and the Sacraments*, 34.

and practices that constitute proper human sociality. When Christians know and live this polity, their words and actions affect other social orders and polities around them. As Karl Barth put it in 1946:

> That which took place in history was the activity of the mercy of the one God, which touches every man. . . . Christian ethics is not individualistic. Christian ethics shapes community, the community of Christians, first of all, the community of those who have heard this call. But Christian ethics cannot allow men outside the community of Christians to cut themselves off or construct some sort of party. It can only form community also outside: the civil community. Christian ethics in its entirety repeats [God's] summons to service. Christian ethics is not aristocratic, knows no royalty, no sovereignty of leader or master other than that which consists in a man being at the disposal of other men, as one link in a chain, as a Christian among Christians, as a brother among brothers.[10]

Joshua Hordern pictures the transposition of these affections from the worshipping community to others. He imagines joy in the saving work of Christ transposed into joy for the 'common goods of society's life, such as harvest, marriage, children, voluntary social care, state welfare provision and peaceful neighbourhoods'—perhaps to 'disturb, renew or correct patterns of [unjust] social trust'.[11] He imagines us learning, in our praises, to participate 'in the great doxology that creation already is',[12] and with a joy that 'makes no pact with scarcity'.[13] The affections of this worshipping community discover consensus in conflict and teach fidelity, 'to support and critique governmental authority amidst the scepticism and alienation of the twenty-first century West'.[14]

Hence it has not been hard to recognise the ripples of Christians' polity into the polities of their neighbours. Christian diaconal care became general care for the vulnerable. The majority of Catholics

---
[10] Karl Barth, 'Christian Ethics', in *God Here and Now* (London: Routledge, 2003), 112–13.
[11] Joshua Hordern, *Political Affections: Civic Participation and Moral Theology* (Oxford: Oxford University Press, 2013), 271.
[12] Hordern, (2013), *Affections,* citing Brock, 276 n.78.
[13] Hordern, (2013), *Affections*, 274.
[14] Hordern, (2013), *Affections*, 293.

and Protestants found how to recognise a *common* good, overcoming sectarianism and giving rise to trade unions. Better conceptions of the 'market' understood it as that which organises our sharing in the service of our neighbour, with correlate restraints. The abolition of evils such as slavery or institutional racism had some origins in Christian conceptions of *imago dei* and ecclesially-derived 'brotherhood'. There are no bright clear lines where theological motivations stop and where the surrounding community finds new affections and objects of love. But such ripples happen regularly enough to motivate new Christian political engagements.

However, the *way* in which the best polity of the church affects other polities nearby is far from clear or settled. In what follows, I will use a provisional typology of public faith to tease out how these kinds of Christian affections might make their mark.

1. Interlude: on typology

Typologies are a risky business. All typologies must be provisional, since none can finally account for every complexity and each can only capture moods we may recognise or contest. Max Weber conceived of the use of 'ideal-types' as deliberately exaggerated abstractions that help to order social data in meaningful ways. They can only be measured in terms of 'adequacy', will satisfy no positivist, and can never account for every historical circumstance. Nevertheless, they act as a unifying analytical construct to accentuate points of view inherent within clusters of concrete phenomena.[15]

Among theologians, the most famous set of ideal types for the relations of Christians to culture are those proposed by H Richard Niebuhr.[16] He conceives of five kinds of interaction between 'Christ' and 'culture':

---

[15] See further Sung Ho Kim, 'Max Weber' §5.2 in *Stanford Encyclopaedia of Philosophy*, at < http://plato.stanford.edu/entries/weber/#IdeTyp>. Accessed 31 May 2016. I thank Bernard Doherty for remembering this mode of social knowledge in Weber.

[16] Helmut Richard Neibuhr, *Christ and Culture* (San Francisco: Harper & Row, 1951). I appreciate the summary by Justin Lewis-Anthony, *If You Meet George Herbert On The Road . . . Kill Him! Radically rethinking priestly ministry* (London: Continuum, 2009), 111–119. My list here includes some terms borrowed from Lewis-Anthony, Timothy Gorringe, and an earlier work by

First Extreme: 'The Christ of Culture':
'Conformist', 'Natural Law' or 'Accommodationist' type.

Median 1: 'Christ above Culture':
'Synthetic' or 'Architectonic' type.

Median 2: 'Christ and Culture in Paradox':
'Dualist' or 'Oscillatory' type.

Median 3: 'Christ the Transformer of Culture':
'Crisis' or 'Conversionist' type.

Second Extreme: 'Christ against Culture':
'Oppositional' or 'New Law' type.

This influential typology still retains some resonances. However it has been critiqued for a 'monolithic' view of culture that excludes the possibility that 'someone might reject some part of culture, affirm other parts of culture and seek to transform yet another part'.[17] My own difficulty with it lies in clarifying what distinguishes those 'median' positions.

2. Four primal postures

I propose a more granular typology. It begins with four primal moral postures of response to others. I call these 'cooperation', 'subversion', 'exposure' and 'separation'. I will simply observe these as they appear in the Bible, with a slightly longer treatment on the less familiar notion of 'subversion'.

Cooperation: Christians often straightforwardly cooperate with the plans and purposes of others as an 'everyday' posture. 'If it is possible, as far as it depends on you, live at peace with everyone' (Romans 12:18). The New Testament slave can willingly assist the master, precisely because Christ has become the true Master (Ephesians 6:5–9; Colossians 3:22–23; 1 Timothy 6:1–2), and the master a new kind of equal. Peter exhorts cooperation with human expressions of authority (literally, 'every human creation', 1 Peter 2:13), just as the prophet Jeremiah could exhort Jewish exiles to seek Babylon's welfare

---
H. R. Niebuhr.
[17] Lewis-Anthony, (2009), *If You Meet George Herbert*, 118.

(Jeremiah 29:7). Cooperation can represent mere co-option. But I have in mind the intentionality that arises when another's plans and purposes are coincident with the Christian's inhabitation of the world as a creature under God's purposes for it.

Subversion describes an unnerving kind of cooperation that participates alongside another, while also challenging some basic frames and motivations. A Christian may respond to contempt with hopeful gentleness (1 Peter 3:14–16), or to wariness with grace (Colossians 4:5–6). Subversion inserts reconciliation into discourses of revenge, abundance into discourses of scarcity, and affirmation of the unrecognised within discourses of merit. While formally cooperative, it materially destabilises the established polity. Christian subversives eschew the usual set-piece frontal assaults that typify much political disputing. We may press the Austrian philosopher Wittgenstein into service here, to illustrate:

> We must begin with the mistake and transform it into what is true. That is, we must uncover the source of the error; otherwise hearing what is true won't help us. It cannot penetrate . . . To convince someone of what is true, it is not enough to state it; we must find the road from error to truth. I must plunge again and again in the water of doubt.[18]

When someone quietly observes an established ideology for a time and discerns the passions that drive it, they may succeed to insert a new affection into the discourse. The immediate result will be doubt and confusion about the old frame of reference.

Oliver O'Donovan's portrayal of the threefold order of ministry offers a small cameo of subversion.[19] The close-quarters, grass roots engagements of the diaconate show that to *be* society is to share. These engagements subvert 'prevailing patterns of social standing and honour' and 'redirect. . . resources counter to popular social valuations'. The presbyterate confesses 'the authority of God's word in the context of its place'. It does not 'wait on the threat of actual damage

---

[18] Ludwig Wittgenstein, *Remarks on Frazer's Golden Bough*, edited by Rush Rhees, translated by A. C. Miles, (Nottinghamshire: Brynmill, 1979), 11e.

[19] Oliver O'Donovan, *The Ways of Judgment: The Bampton Lectures, 2003* (Grand Rapids: Eerdmans, 2005), 291–92 for all quotations in this paragraph.

and harm' but warns and counsels of future judgment. Hence a local church community may no longer merely endorse local traditions, but 'takes tradition seriously precisely as those aspects of its common life for which it is immediately responsible, where the judgments of God's kingdom are to be revealed.' The episcopate teaches a church 'not to confine its deliberations to the local, national, linguistic or racial spheres, but to explore contested issues in a catholic manner, not only attending to Christians from every present source, but also from every past age'. Bishops assist the church to become the polity that blocks a society from thinking it can 'export its local assumptions and values en masse', so restraining it 'from universalising its own local experiences and perspectives.' In all these ways and more, an effective church will 'forward the social good which [political societies] exist to defend.' That such moments seem historically uncommon does not negate the possibilities of subversion.

Exposure is whistleblowing polemic. For St Paul in 1 Corinthians 5, exposure is not the primary posture for relating to different others (1 Corinthians 5:9–10, 12), and it appears infrequently in the New Testament letters. But it has roots in Old Testament prophecy (such as the 'watchman' metaphor of Ezekiel 3:16–19 and 33:1–9); in the polemical aspects of Jesus' ministry (Matthew 23:12–35; Luke 6:42–52); and in the exposure of 'fruitless works of darkness' (Ephesians 5:11–14). Such moments of exposure seem to have been the flashpoint for the outright disagreements and return expressions of contempt seen in the starkly polarised communities of 1 Peter 4:3–4 (a text that also hints at the next posture, separation).

Separation appears in the New Testament (2 Corinthians 6:17–7:1) as warrant for a 'monastic' strategy. The separation motif cannot successfully be encoded as a simple set of rules of disengagement. Rather, it avoids the passive compliance in some habitual social evil that occurs simply because our moral imagination fails to envisage *leaving* the group that sponsors it. When the apostles declare 'we must obey God rather than any human authority' (Acts 5:29; cf. 4:19–20), they serve notice that they are taking a different path. Others must then determine whether to oppose them, join them or leave them alone.

It may be lived literally and geographically, such as in a dark-ages monastery, a modern Christian school, a hospice, a non-usurious microfinancing initiative, or a home for pregnant women who wish to keep their children. Such communities can operate as islands of life shaped by the gospel. But in the light of Paul's passing remark that Christians do not voluntarily 'leave the world' (1 Corinthians 5:10b), this posture cannot be the default. At most, separation is an emergency condition.

These four primal moral postures represent context-dependent discernment, often enacted by individuals and small groups in various cultural transactions. They help form our response to a given issue: will we uphold the rules of some cultural practice, or destabilise and renovate the practice, or attempt to bring it down, or leave it to begin a different practice? It may be that each of us has a preferred response, and that we tend to erect systems of justification to defend our favourite. It may follow that we each might experiment with less-favoured options to use as the times require.

These four primal moral postures are scalable. We can deploy them in a personal relationship, in a small group, in a workplace, or in response to authority.

3. Four reactions to government

There are many modes of presence in a community, and many audiences to address. Individual Christians bear verbal and practical witness in workplaces. They gather in parachurch or secular organisations of conscience. Local churches organise for various causes. Denominational representatives comment and advocate for this or that. James Beckford's pioneering work on new religious movements introduced the concept of their 'modes of insertion in society for the purpose of producing and reproducing the conditions of their collective mission.'[20] Finding such 'modes of insertion' could valuably amplify any analysis of public faith, which is unfortunately beyond my scope. Here it suffices simply to observe that any practical political theology inevitably terminates upon *the public Christian's address to government*.

---

[20] James Beckford, *Cult Controversies: The Societal Response to New Religious Movements* (London and New York: Tavistock, 1985), 81. I am indebted to my colleague Bernard Doherty for this insight.

A Christian's position in relation to various social 'issues' and their address to government often combine to become a fixation on *policy*, where most public theology paddles about for better and worse. Policy-fixation elides other matters that might fruitfully claim the public theologian's attention, such as structural dysfunctions in political institutions; or the hidden lines of power whose magnetic fields twist and distort the polity; or the collusion between media mediocrity and the disengaged, self-interest fetishism of voters that robs political discourse of any traction and forces politicians to present us with their worst-self. Furthermore, the public theologian will sweat about whether he or she is a 'representative' or not, particularly when churches include people who would espouse 'left' and 'right' views. These meta-issues all deserve closer attention.

But for now, let us simply consider four styles of operation in relation to government that Christians often deploy: 'translation', 'demarcation', 'embodiment' and 'restoration'. Each discloses some predisposition on the legitimacy and limits of governmental authority (although again, political agents do not all fit neatly into these 'ideal types').

'Translation' accommodates to government and attempts to converse with government by commending Christian concerns in the terms of others' concerns. In our time and place, theology takes its place in the Rawlsian project of justificatory liberalism as an exercise of translation, and is most often seen in the work of established or pseudo-established churches. As sociologist of religion Peter Berger puts it, 'traditional religious affirmations are translated into terms appropriate to the new frame of reference . . . Different translation grammars have been employed for this purpose'.[21] The former Archbishop of Canterbury (1942–44) William Temple's principle-based approach is typical:

> The method of the Church's impact upon society at large should be twofold. The Church must announce Christian principles and point out where the existing social order at any time is in conflict with them. It must then pass on to Christian citizens, acting in their civic capacity, the task of re-shaping the existing order in closer conformity to the principles.[22]

---

[21] Peter Berger, *A Rumour of Angels* (Harmondsworth: Penguin, 1969), 34.
[22] William Temple, *Christianity and Social Order* (London: Shepheard-Walwyn, 1976), 58.

Ronald Preston uses the term 'middle axiom' to picture these principles at work.[23] Examples include that 'the government has the responsibility of maintaining full employment';[24] 'private centres of economic power should not be stronger than the government';[25] and 'every citizen should have a voice in the conduct of the business of industry which is carried on by means of his labour.'[26]

Preston can think of eight advantages in middle axioms, two of which are that they 'give the Christian community something to say relevant to the concerns of the general public',[27] and that 'they help the church to avoid... never [having] a relevant word... in structures of life in which God has placed us alongside others of all faiths with whom we have to work, and which cannot presuppose a shared Christian faith as a basis for their working.'[28]

Both these 'advantages' suppose that theology cannot be 'relevant', as when he concludes that a middle-axiom method 'takes the religious overtones out of politics',[29] a response to secularisation (or secularism) that we immediately recognise. The method becomes inexorably atheological by design, and complies with Sidgwick's famous programmatic Enlightenment slogan: 'Principles will soon be everything, and tradition nothing'.[30]

The possibility of a persuasive translation will rely upon some conception of natural law. We do share a divinely ordered cosmos, and Christians can speak intelligibly about what they think others may have missed. But as Christian political philosopher Jonathan Chaplin puts it, natural law cannot function to justify positive laws. It only explains why consensus sometimes emerges. But when it does emerge and how far it extends is entirely contingent: consensus is episodic and fragile.[31]

---

[23] Ronald H. Preston, 'Middle Axioms in Christian Social Ethics', in *Social Christianity: A Reader*, edited by John Atherton (London: SPCK, 1994), 149.
[24] Temple, (1976), *Christianity and Social Order*, 8.
[25] Temple, (1976), *Christianity and Social Order*, 8.
[26] Temple; cited in John Stott, *New Issues Facing Christians Today* (London: Marshall Pickering, 1999), 221.
[27] Preston, (1994), 'Middle Axioms', 149.
[28] Preston, (1994), 'Middle Axioms', 150.
[29] Preston, (1994), 'Middle Axioms', 152.
[30] Cited in David Fergusson, 'Communitarianism and Liberalism: Towards a Convergence?' *Studies in Christian Ethics* 10/1 (1997): 38.
[31] Email correspondence between Chaplin and the author.

We can find translationists leveraging this consensus while also adopting the primal moral postures, to give translational cooperation, subversion, exposure and separation. The public theologian dances between the need to speak accessibly and so 'translate' to a degree, and the drift toward programmatic unbelief. But the naïve idealism of the principle-based, and their failure to notice the loves and hates that skew the perceptions of the populace, offer little when democracy turns beastly.

'Demarcation' asserts cultural space under government by supposedly distinguishing Christian concerns from others' concerns.

In his *City of God*, Augustine pictures the two 'cities' of God and of earth mingled together, competing for cultural space in a complex myriad of ways. In Augustine's thinking, one cannot easily 'demarcate' the two cities. But Michael Banner points out how Luther's use of this motif demarcated boundaries between the spiritual and secular realms, based on their different roles and functions, and in a way Augustine never intended. This resulted, says Banner, in morality being 'lost, not found, beyond the law.'[32] In other words, Augustine's two intermingled cities later hardened into the so-called rules of 'ecclesial' and 'civil' swords, two strongly demarcated realms of authority. A very contestable reading of the dominical word about 'rendering to Caesar' (Matthew 22:17–21) becomes the proof-text for this view.

In this way of thinking, 'demarcating' consists in settling upon areas where Christians have no intention to influence anything versus no-go areas no government may touch. The so-called 'wall' of separation; skirmishes over the religious speaker's 'right' to 'impose values'; and the attempt to define religion into a privatised space of interior authority alone, all continue this impulse.

Ironically, it is often clergy as much as 'secularists' who expend much energy on demarcation, sometimes in an effort to clarify the 'core business' of their difficult and complex vocation. The version of conservative evangelicalism I know takes as its 'core business' the formation of biblically and theologically literate churches. In an odd non-sequitur, that somehow becomes the 'core business' of each church member, who are often not encouraged in others forms of

---

[32] Michael Banner, *Christian Ethics: A Brief History* (Chichester: Wiley-Blackwell, 2009), 70.

social engagement. On this view, there can be no serious address to the structures of society other than polemical broadsides against society's folly. This mood is marked in these circles by perennial discussions demarcating evangelism against so-called 'social action'—an undifferentiated category covering many kinds of engagement ranging from social welfare provision to political advocacy.

Of course, authoritative competence does require humility. An Australian Foreign Minister, Alexander Downer—who was, admittedly, enforcing some demarcation from the political side—lampooned senior clergy from whom 'political and social judgements are delivered with magisterial certainty while utterances on fundamental Christian doctrines are characterised by scepticism and doubt'.[33] At its best, the Dooyeweerdian conception of 'sphere sovereignty' describes how material competencies in this or that area of life constitute inherent forms of authority that should be respected. A proper demarcation of the two cities may house expressions of cooperation, subversion, exposure and separation.

But as a theological project, the costs are prohibitive, and the results can be catastrophic. (Banner points to the egregious quietism of pre-war German Christians as his case in point.[34])

'*Embodiment*' stands aside from government, and attempts simply to live Christian concerns on Christian terms. This ecclesial communitarianism extends the Anabaptist tradition via the Macintyrean insight (as paraphrased by David Fergusson) that 'the ends we seek cannot be understood except by reference to the practises, communities and traditions we inhabit. The Enlightenment project of seeking to establish morality on grounds independent of the particular claims of a tradition is therefore doomed from the outset.'[35]

Stanley Hauerwas' trademark assertion therefore follows: 'Put starkly, the first social ethical task of the church is to be the church . . . the church does not have a social ethic; the church is a social ethic.'[36] The anti-foundationalism of this position makes it impossible,

---

[33] The Hon. Alexander Downer, 'Sir Thomas Playford Annual Lecture 2003' at <www.foreignminister.gov.au/speeches/2003/030827_playford.html>.Accessed 25 November 2015.
[34] Banner, (2009), *Brief History*, 56.
[35] Fergusson, (1997), 'Communitarianism and Liberalism', 34.
[36] Stanley Hauerwas, *The Peaceable Kingdom* (Notre Dame: University of Notre Dame Press, 1983), 99.

by definition, to *translate* theology into any shared middle axioms, and expects that the only serious effect a church can have on its surrounding polity is by the inhabitation of counter-cultural witness.

In terms of the four primal postures, 'embodiment' would seem only to express separation. But Hauerwas's notoriously unscholastic, hit-and-run polemic—and the fact that *Time* magazine could portray him in 2001 as 'America's Best Theologian'—hides in plain sight that the Word is *not* unintelligible to those within other forms of life. It therefore becomes easier to conceive of cooperative, subversive and exposing instances of 'embodiment'.

'Restoration' asserts divine authority over government and attempts to re-establish Christian concerns as other's concerns. I have in mind movements ranging from Greg Bahnsen's theonomist reconstructionism[37] through to the much softer-edged 'biblical relationism' of the UK's Michael Schluter and Jubilee Centre/ Relationships Foundation.[38] The US, UK and Australia all have lively conservative advocacy groups who defend and promote some version of a Christian heritage or a return to 'Christian values', usually by resisting or promoting new legislation. While they resort to various kinds of principle-based translation, at the base of their appeal is that the nation is constitutively Christian and should be held to whatever formal Christian elements are found in the origins of the polity's institutions. We could find restorationist versions of cooperation, subversion, exposure and separation.

It does remains incumbent upon the public theologian to describe back to the polity the Christian traditions and practices that helped form its political intuitions and imagination. This has been the burden of Oliver O'Donovan's political theology. Whereas Hauerwas rejects restorationist projects as the last dregs of an always illicit Constantinianism, O'Donovan has set out to show how theology's long tradition of reflection upon society gave rise to early modern

---

[37] Greg L. Bahnsen, 'The Theonomic Reformed Approach to Law and Gospel,' in *Five Views on Law and Gospel*, edited by Stanley N. Gundry (Grand Rapids: Zondervan, 1996). Christopher JH Wright summarises some objections to this project in his *Old Testament Ethics for the People of God* (Leicester: IVP, 2004), 403–08.

[38] Michael Schluter and John Ashcroft (editors), *Jubilee Manifesto: a framework, agenda & strategy for Christian social reform*, (Leicester: InterVarsity Press, 2005), *passim;* Wright, *Old Testament Ethics*, 408–11.

liberalism and its political institutions. The ballast of O'Donovan's work is deeply conservative, but he is no restorationist. As he puts it, 'the Christian state may be disclosed from time to time as a sign of the Kingdom, disappearing at one moment to return at another. . . What it could not do, of course, would be to protect its arrangements against constitutional reform'[39] because that would be to short-circuit the church's task of mission to each new generation.

4. The affections of Christian polity

The plethora of Christian responses to the wider polity springs from various Christian affections, and can't be made to fit some grand theory of how we move from Christian polity to those that surround us. (The expectation that it should might simply disclose that we are uncritically beholden to some version of justificatory liberalism.) This provisional typology may open up surprising new options for engagement. It also offers some understanding of others' attempts at public faith, whether or not we agree with them.

Once I have settled whether cooperation, subversion, exposure or separation is called for on some issue, I can then imagine what a translationist, demarcationist, embodied or restorationist expression of it might look like. The process forces me to weigh the passions and affections that drive me, and so perhaps to expand my political imagination. I may immediately reject some options, but may also unveil liberty to move between modes of engagement as the situation demands.

The views of others may also be described along these two axes of primal moral evaluation, and reaction to government. I suspect, for example, that Christian disagreement about human rights law has in part been a fight between cooperative translationism and demarcated separatism. I wonder if this two-axis typology, or some version of it, might serve to identify other confusions in that plurality of Christian response.

---

[39] Oliver O'Donovan, *The Desire of the Nations: Rediscovering the Roots of Political Theology* (Cambridge: Cambridge University Press, 1998), 224.

I am finally tempted to suggest that there may remain something good about that pluralism of Christian engagement, despite its inefficiencies for coherent policy formation. Perhaps the better moments of each Christian engagement arise from exigencies of the moment, beginning in subject-to-subject relations, in responses arising from the affections, where Hamann began; but in this case, from affections that have been formed through worship. For engagements that spring from worship are better than no engagement, and are in truth the beginnings of a *practical* political theology.

Chapter Five

Faith and the Political: Former Prime Minister Tony Abbott

John Warhurst

Introduction

There are many varieties of faith and of politics. But 'Captain Catholic', former Prime Minister Tony Abbott, is so identified with Catholic/ Christian faith that he makes an obvious case study. For some his experience can be read as evidence of the incompatibility of faith and politics in a secular Australia. For others this experience is evidence rather of the travails of a particular type of Christian leader which should not be generalised. I tend to fall into the latter category.

My observations are rooted not just in this one case but in the opportunity I was given in the first six months of 2010, when Kevin Rudd was Prime Minister, by the Australian Prime Ministers Centre, Museum of Australian Democracy, in Canberra to examine the faith of all 25 (at the time) Australian Prime Ministers and to see how it intersected with politics. We have had three more Prime Ministers since then, Julia Gillard, Tony Abbott and now Malcolm Turnbull. Each of them is a case study in the matter of faith and politics. Abbott's political career has been defined by his battles with Rudd (two wins, in 2010 and 2013), Gillard (a close loss in 2010 and a win in 2013) and Turnbull (a win in 2009 and ultimately the greatest loss of all in 2015).

When I was first conducting research on *The Faith of Australian Prime Ministers* in 2010, Abbott didn't qualify although he had just become Opposition Leader. He loomed then as a fascinating case study which fell outside the brief of my fellowship.[1] Since then he has held the office of Prime Minister for not quite two years from September 2013 to September 2015.

---
[1] John Warhurst, *The Faith of Australian Prime Ministers*, Australian Political Studies Association, Melbourne, 2010.

It was Rudd then who had generated community interest in faith and the political. A Catholic turned Anglican (sort of, anyway) Rudd had made faith in politics his personal political project. He identified himself publicly as a Christian and saw the return of Christians to the Labor fold after the 2004 election defeat as essential to a Labor victory in 2007. Rudd even formed a Labor parliamentary working group to prosecute this aim. He was probably successful and when in office he paraded his church attendance for all to see.[2]

Gillard, Australia's first atheist, rather than agnostic, Prime Minister after deposing Rudd in July 2010, proved an instructive comparison with Rudd because she shared many of his conservative social policy positions despite her declared lack of Christian faith. This called into question many of the assumptions Rudd's critics made about the inevitable consequences of being a Christian or a person of faith in politics. For instance, Gillard was personally opposed to same-sex marriage at the time, as was Rudd, and gave the Australian Christian Lobby the same assurances about their religious concerns, including the maintenance of the federal government's chaplaincy program in schools.[3]

My conclusion then was that the role of faith in politics was often exaggerated since examples of its direct positive impact are difficult to find and, secondly, individuals with vastly different faith experiences can end up with very similar policy positions.

Abbott's successor, Malcolm Turnbull, also a Catholic, has added another perspective which has strengthened this conclusion. Turnbull has a track record on matters like same-sex marriage which shows him to be more liberal than not just Abbott, the fellow Catholic, but also Gillard, the atheist, and Rudd the Anglican, at least when they were in office. Of course Rudd in his second coming and Gillard in retirement changed their minds.

---

[2] John Warhurst, "Religion", *Australian Cultural History*, 28 (1), April 2010.
[3] John Warhurst, 'Religion in the 2010 Election', Julia 2010: *The Caretaker Election*, Editors, Marian Simms and John Wanna (Canberra, ANU E-Press, 2012).

Tony Abbott's Expressions of his Faith

Faith is essentially a private matter and I can't claim to speak authoritatively for the former Prime Minister. Faith can also be expressed in various ways and, unlike Rudd, Abbott did not express himself through frequent public church-going. But in other ways he presented himself to the public as a conservative, orthodox Catholic, educated by the Jesuits at St Ignatius College Riverview and tied closely to his church. He has written about some of these things in his come-back book, *Battlelines*, (2009), and spoken about them on many other occasions.[4]

There are seven elements to this image. I haven't included Abbott 'the Jesuit' though that has generated a literature of its own, because it is seen by some people as almost a sub-set of Catholicism. That identification undoubtedly sends out various messages to the community about this connection to a Catholic GPS school, especially given so much commentary about so many Jesuit-educated Catholics in the Abbott government.[5] There were at least five.

There are so many representations of his Catholic persona that they have to be peeled off like the layers of an onion. Some would be shared with other Catholic leaders, but he has so many that as a Catholic leader he cannot be replicated. He is certainly not a representative Catholic leader, although as Bob Dixon has shown, the idea of a representative Catholic in a diverse Australian Church is impossible.[6]

First, Abbott had studied for several years to be a priest at the Catholic seminary in Sydney. This step was a signal to the electorate of his religious enthusiasm even though he eventually took a different path. He is still often referred to as a former seminarian.

Secondly, he rated the Catholic activist, B. A. 'Bob' Santamaria as one of his most important mentors and in a famous formulation proclaimed that the Democratic Labor Party (DLP) was 'alive and well within the Howard government'.[7] By this Abbott meant, if you look closely at the context, that on socio-moral issues like anti-abortion and

---

[4] Tony Abbott, *Battlelines* (Melbourne, Melbourne University Press, 2009).
[5] GPS – Greater Public School.
[6] See Chapter Three, 'Post-Secularity and Australian Catholics', Bob Dixon.
[7] Abbott, (2009), *Battlelines*, 11.

anti-pornography the Liberals were carrying on DLP campaigns, but it was perceived as a more general statement of the state of play with Abbott a standard bearer of Catholic DLP values.[8]

Thirdly, as Minister for Health he put a focus on lowering abortion rates and opposed the introduction of the anti-abortion pill RU-486. This controversy was to lead to a cross-party bill sponsored by four women Senators and passed on a conscience vote, which removed ministerial power over such regulations.[9] These episodes tagged him as an activist, anti-abortion political leader.

Fourthly, after becoming Prime Minister he set himself against any attempt to introduce legislation in support of same-sex marriage. He even opposed a conscience vote for Coalition MPs. One of his final acts as PM was to announce that a plebiscite would be held on same-sex marriage at some stage after the next federal election. Abbott came to be seen, including by some in his own party, as the major impediment to this reform. He led from the front again.[10]

Fifthly, Abbott portrayed himself as being close to the official church. Anti-Catholicism in Australia has always emphasised church direction of Catholic MPs as a quintessentially Catholic thing, along with notions of a 'Catholic vote'. Abbott presented himself on the cover of a popular weekend magazine holding a portrait of Pope Benedict about the time of World Youth Day in Sydney.[11] But more importantly he was seen as very close to Cardinal George Pell, Archbishop of Sydney. In one famous example, in the middle of the 2004 election campaign debate about state aid, he described Cardinal Pell as his spiritual adviser.[12] Pell represented the conservative face of Catholicism in Australia and the identification would not have boosted Abbott's popularity in the community.

---

[8] John Warhurst, "Revising the idea of Santamaria as Tony Abbott's mentor", *Eureka Street*, 31 August 2015.
[9] John Warhurst, Conscience Votes in the Australia Federal Parliament, *Australian Journal of Politics and History*, 54 (4), December 2008.
[10] Wayne Errington and Peter Van Onselen, *Battleground* (Melbourne: Melbourne University Press, 2015), 186-188.
[11] Tony Abbott, The Mission-Benedict and Us, Weekend Magazine, *The Australian*, 14 June 2008.
[12] John Warhurst, 'Religion in 21st Century Australian National Politics', *Papers on Parliament*, 46, December 2006.

Sixthly, there was his attitude towards women in public life (though whether this is tied to his faith may be disputed). This perception has been encapsulated in two events. There was Gillard's famous 'misogynist' speech to the Parliament in October 2012, which was directed squarely at Abbott.[13] Then, after becoming Prime Minister in September 2013, there was his creation of a 20 person Cabinet which included just one woman. This was clearly at odds with community standards, yet Abbott was not for turning and, even worse, seemed oblivious to the problem. He did very little to repair the situation, even though he had a limited reshuffle of his ministry in December 2014.

Finally, and this is something I have become more aware of since his removal from office, though it is also contained in his maiden speech, has been his deliberate use of religious language. Some religious language has entered everyday speech but Abbott goes beyond the norm. The final words of his farewell speech as PM (echoing his maiden speech) were:

> The reverend Richard Johnson took as his text 'What shall I render unto the Lord for all his blessings to me?' At this, my final statement as Prime Minister, I say: I have rendered all and I am proud of my service. My love for this country is as strong as ever and may God bless this great Commonwealth. Thank you.[14]

Then, more recently, there was his key note address at the second annual Margaret Thatcher Lecture in London. As reported by two incredulous journalists Nick Miller and Latika Bourke:

> The professed Catholic, surprisingly, spoke against one of Jesus' greatest commandments. 'The imperative to "love your neighbour as yourself" is at the heart of every Western polity... but right now this wholesome instinct is leading much of Europe into catastrophic error'.[15]

---

[13] *Sydney Morning Herald*, 10 October 2012.
[14] *Sydney Morning Herald*, 15 September 2015.
[15] Nick Miller and Latika Bourke, *Sydney Morning Herald*, 29 October 2015.

This statement was condemned by Catholic priest Fr Frank Brennan, and Bishop Pat Power, and its meaning has been debated subsequently by Christian theologians.[16]

Media Representations of Abbott's Faith

There is no doubt that the media, including political cartoonists, made fun of Abbott's faith (and of course of his name). He was treated unkindly. He became known not only as 'Captain Catholic' but even more unkindly as the 'mad monk'. Defenders of the former Prime Minister claim that he was treated in a way no other political leader of faith, including no other Catholic leader, has been. And there have been many other Catholic leaders, including not just Turnbull but also Dr Brendan Nelson as well as state and territory leaders. Some commentators, including Gerard Henderson, have even seen this treatment of Abbott as an indication of not just partisanship but of old-fashioned anti-Catholicism.[17]

Abbott was a cartoonists dream (and cartoonists can be cruel) and it must be remembered that the religious Abbott was only one of several images conjured up by cartoonists. Before the religious Abbott there was Abbott the head-kicker and I own an original cartoon in this vein by Ian Sharpe of the *Canberra Times*, in which Abbott is drawn as a grinning hob-nail boot. Pre-religion there was also Abbott the 'young fogey', which captured an enduring image of the man as an old-fashioned, almost pre-modern figure, out of kilter with the times.[18]

After the' religious Abbott', there came the common representation of Abbott as the fitness fanatic and life-saver. The image of him in brief 'budgie smugglers' may turn about to be the image that prevails in future years. The former PM was not represented then just as a man of faith but in many other guises.

---

[16] *Sydney Morning Herald*, 29 October 2015.
[17] See in general on the relationship between Abbott and Santamaria, Gerard Henderson, *Santamaria: A Most Unusual Man*, (Melbourne: Melbourne University Press, 2015), 296-303.
[18] Paul Keating in *Brisbane Times*, 26 November 2007.

Tony Abbott's Reaction to the Faith of Rudd and Gillard

As Opposition Leader, Abbott took it upon himself to fight Rudd's representation of himself as a Christian leader. In a famous article in *The Monthly* in October 2006 entitled 'Faith in Politics' Rudd identified himself as a being in a long tradition of Christian Socialism within the Labor Party. He presented Labor as the party of the Social Gospel.[19]

Abbott would have none of that and criticised Christian Socialism as a fraud and Rudd, to the extent that he was a Christian, as being unrepresentative of Labor values anyway. In *Battlelines*, he asserted that on matters like 'foreign aid for third world abortions', Labor's 'secular humanist instincts reassert themselves' and that 'Christian voters are likely to find Rudd's 'I didn't like it, but I couldn't stop it' response, particularly lame'.[20]

However, once he was faced with Gillard rather than Rudd, Abbott became more circumspect. There was notably little attempt to contrast Abbott the Christian with Gillard the atheist. This was wise as to do so would have been counter-productive, playing into a narrow and unproductive image of the then Opposition Leader.

The same is true of Abbott's presentation of himself during his two years as Prime Minister, a period dominated by foreign policy concerns and a belligerent image of him summed up as the man who would shirtfront Russian President Vladimir Putin. During this time one notable development was the election of his NSW Liberal colleague, Mike Baird, as Premier of NSW. Baird, a political leader who had studied theology and considered a life in the evangelical ministry, offered an alternative model of a political leader of public faith. They were from different Christian traditions, of course, but the contrast showed that the Abbott way was not the only way within the Liberal Party.[21]

---

[19] Reprinted in Robert Macklin, *Kevin Rudd: The Biography* (Melbourne: Viking, 2007).
[20] Abbott, (2009), *Battlelines*, 181.
[21] John Warhurst, "State elections the biggest opinion poll of all, *Eureka Street*. 3 March 2015.

Faith and Public Policy

There was always very little chance, despite the claims of his extreme critics such as Susan Mitchell, that Abbott's faith would dictate the approach of his government other than in a narrow band of socio-moral concerns such as abortion and same sex marriage.[22] Study of previous prime ministers show that faith can encourage a life of public service as well as inspiring a commitment to social justice, even among agnostics such as Bob Hawke.[23] But it is hard to point to specific public policy outcomes of a major kind.

Among previous Catholic Prime Ministers, such as James Scullin and Joe Lyons, it is notable how they steered away from their church's primary public policy goal, state aid for private schools or educational justice as the church described it. Rather it was the Presbyterian Sir Robert Menzies and the agnostic Gough Whitlam who were responsible for its introduction, with nudging by the DLP. The unspoken agreement within both major parties was that Catholic PMs should not be 'too Catholic' in their inclinations.[24]

In Abbott's case, John Howard had kept him in check in this regard. Some of Abbott's Cabinet colleagues under Howard, including Peter Costello, may have been concerned that Abbott was 'channelling Santa' by not being enough of a champion of free enterprise.[25] But they were not so worried by Abbott's more directly Catholic beliefs.

In office, Abbott was surrounded by Cabinet colleagues, many of whom, including Treasurer Joe Hockey, were Catholics too. Some of them, like Kevin Andrews, had policy preferences that could be traced to their faith. In Andrews' case, as Minister for Social Services, it was relationships counselling which found its expression in government policy.[26] But there was little chance of a more full-blown Christian government.

What did happen, however, was that Abbott was held to so-called Christian standards on his signature policy of 'stopping the boats'.

---

[22] Susan Mitchell, *Tony Abbott: A Man's Man* (Melbourne: Penguin, 2011).
[23] Warhurst, *The Faith of Australian Prime Ministers*; Roy Williams, *In God They Trust* (Bible Society, Sydney, 2013).
[24] Warhurst, (2013), *The Faith of Australian Prime Ministers*.
[25] Abbott, (2009), *Battlelines*, 11.
[26] *Sydney Morning Herald* 3 August 2014.

This is an example of the higher standards to which self-proclaimed Christians are often held. When they stick to their Christian positions on moral matters they are criticised for doing so, but equally, when they fall short of so-called standards of compassion (not to mention personal morality) they are condemned as hypocrites.

Abbott was condemned by Christians and non-Christians alike for his stance on asylum seekers and refugees. I have seen a predominantly Catholic audience warm to Abbott on abortion but become decidedly cool on asylum seeker policy. He was clearly sensitive to this when framing his advice to European political leaders on their response to asylum seekers.

In an interesting twist, the views of the Jesuit Pope Francis, on refugees and particularly on the environment in his encyclical *Laudato Si*, were also interpreted as posing a particular problem for Abbott and other conservative Catholic leaders around the world. As Catholics, they were expected to take their Pope seriously, but they did not.[27]

Faith and Advancement within the Major Political Parties

Do men and women of public faith, like Abbott, find it difficult to advance within our major political parties?

Almost certainly that is not the case. Neither Abbott nor Baird had any difficulty in advancing within the NSW Liberal Party. The balance of the Abbott Cabinet suggests that other Catholics and other Christians, such as Senator Eric Abetz, then Senate Leader, had no difficulty either. If anything, the presence of Abbott and Baird, shortly after Rudd, could be interpreted as showing that seriously religious leaders were over-represented for a short time in Australian public life.

In fact, religious faith networks can be of assistance as well as teaching politically useful skills to aspiring politicians. The Religious Right is strong within several branches of the Liberal Party and the Lyons Forum, a Christian ginger-group, was influential in the early period of the Howard government.[28] Strong Christians like Tim Fischer and the Anglican John Anderson, especially, have led the

---

[27] John Warhurst, 'Abbott wedged by the Pope?', *The Canberra Times*, 25 June 2016.
[28] Marion Maddox, *God Under Howard*, (Sydney: Allen and Unwin, 2005).

Nationals in recent times and become Deputy Prime Minister. There are many others.

In the case of the Labor Party, a religious faction concentrated around the Shop Assistants Union, led by Joe De Bruyn, is a powerful force. There are fewer Christians in that party now than once was the case in the old 'Catholic' Labor Party, but the Right remains the dominant faction and many within that faction are religious believers who are church affiliated. Former NSW Premier Kristina Keneally is a case in point of a theologically literate, though unorthodox, political leader of faith.

In the past, it was sectarianism which undoubtedly hindered the advancement of Catholics within the Liberal Party. Abbott was the first home-grown Catholic Prime Minister representing a conservative party, followed by Turnbull. The top levels of the Turnbull government still include strong Christians like Christopher Pyne from South Australia and Andrew Robb from Victoria.

Conservative Christian Positions and Modern Politics

Are conservative Christian positions on contentious moral issues likely to hinder a political career? This is a more general question. Public opinion polls regularly show that on issues like opposition to same sex marriage conservative Christians form a minority. On this issue, Abbott was out of step with other conservative leaders around the world, including David Cameron (UK) and John Key (New Zealand). Turnbull is now in step.

The general answer is that being in a minority on contentious and sensitive public issues through taking a conservative Christian/Catholic position can pose electoral difficulties. Wayne Errington and Peter Van Onselen allude to this in their study of Abbott's fall.[29] This is so especially as the number of observant Christians in the community declines. But holding a conservative minority position also brings some strong support from, in the case of Australia, powerful pressure groups such as the Australian Christian Lobby and the Australian Catholic Bishops Conference.

---

[29] Errington and Van Onselen, (2015), *Battleground*, 81-82.

Leaders of faith in this minority conservative position, like Abbott, are forced to present themselves as defenders of traditional rather than modern values. In 2009 Abbott, apparently feeling lonely in this regard, yearned for support within his own senior ranks. As he said somewhat regretfully: 'it might not hurt to have another senior coalition frontbencher taking Christian concerns seriously'.[30]

The Role of Faith in Abbott's Downfall

What role did his Christian faith play in Tony Abbott's downfall?
It almost certainly played little or no direct role. The reasons for his downfall are still being analysed but those advanced so far do not relate directly to his faith.[31]

Rather those reasons included his inability to adapt his approach from opposition to government; his belligerent style and tone; his responsibility for a most unfair and unpopular budget in 2014; his failure to listen to his backbenchers; his over-centralised administration; and his inability to project a forward-looking vision on economic policy. It was the latter weakness that Turnbull seized upon.

These weaknesses all contributed to his consistent personal unpopularity and to the unpopularity of the Abbott government. Turnbull also focused on this point and the Liberal party room, after giving him one warning in March this year, lost faith, of a different kind, that Abbott could lead them to victory in 2016.

Untangling the deeper reasons for Abbott's long-term personal unpopularity is more difficult. Voters, especially women voters, did not like his persona. His faith is part of that persona, but the outward characteristics and policy positions were only indirectly related to that faith. Public faith does not inevitably lead to a personality like Tony Abbott's.

---

[30] Abbott, (2009), *Battlelines*, 181.
[31] Niki Savva, *The Road to Ruin: How Tony Abbott and Peta Credlin destroyed their own government* (Melbourne: Scribe, 2016).

Conclusion

Tony Abbott was defined in part by his Catholic persona, but there was much more to the man than that. Those other characteristics included several of great political significance, such as his governing style and his personal belligerence when in political situations.

The particular Catholic persona he constructed for himself cut both ways in terms of his career. As he rose to prominence, it gave him mentors like Mr Santamaria and Cardinal Pell. It also did him no harm within the NSW Division of the Liberal Party.

While the evidence is mixed, that persona seems to have both attracted and repelled certain classes of voters in the 2010 and 2013 federal elections. Some Catholics certainly gave him their tribal allegiance and this tended to counter-balance the relatively small number of voters who objected specifically to his Christian persona. So it didn't make much difference.[32]

On the negative side, some of his personal characteristics and attitudes, which can arguably be traced to, or were reinforced by, his particular brand of Catholic faith, helped construct him as a narrow and old-fashioned person; in other words, as a young 'old fogey'. These attitudes included his anti-abortion and anti-same sex marriage campaigns, and even perhaps his failure to recognise the talents of women Liberals and his alleged misogyny towards his opponent, Gillard.

When the faith of Australian Prime Ministers is discussed in the future, Abbott and Rudd will be at the centre of those discussions as among the most publicly religious of all the twenty-eight Australian prime ministers. So too will Gillard as one of the least religious. We have lived in an atypical era in that regard.

Australia's longest-serving prime ministers, Menzies and Howard, the conventional Christians, and Hawke, the agnostic, have been closer to the mean by this measure. It may be that easy-going Australians prefer their religion to be served lukewarm and their leaders to be not too dogmatic and not too intense in matters of faith and morals. It remains to be seen how Turnbull emerges in matters of faith but the early signs are that he is more in that acceptable mould.

---

[32] Ian McAllister, 'Warhurst, Religion and the 2010 Election'. *The Australian Voter*, (Sydney: UNSW Press, 2011).

Chapter Six

Emmanuel Levinas: Society, Justice and Mercy

Terry A. Veling

> I am against bigness and greatness in all their forms. The bigger the unit you deal with, the hollower, the more brutal, the more mendacious is the life displayed. So I am against all big organisations as such, national ones first and foremost; against all big successes and big results, and in favour of the eternal forces of truth which always work in the individual and immediately unsuccessful way, under-dogs always, till history comes, after they are long dead, and puts them on top. (Dorothy Day, *The Duty of Delight: Diaries*)

The Question of Social Existence

Emmanuel Levinas (1906–1995) suffered the tragic loss of many of his family members in the Holocaust and was himself incarcerated as a prisoner of war. His writings come to us as a radical attempt to re-envisage the world of religious and ethical thinking in the face of the tragedies of our era. Although he suffered the disastrous effects of collective cruelty, he did not allow the foreboding of those deathly effects to completely overwhelm his thinking. Rather, he turned his thinking to the questions and themes of goodness, ethical responsibility, and being-for-the-other. As one commentator says, 'Levinas is a prophet of the murdered people . . . He is not simply a theorist, but a person responding to the trauma of our time. His ethic is at once an intellectual edifice *and* an extended prayer.'[1]

---

[1] Roger Gottlieb, 'Ethics and Trauma: Levinas, Feminism, and Deep Ecology,' *CrossCurrents* 44/2 (1994), 232-33.

According to Levinas, the face-to-face ethical relation of being-for-the-other is written into the very fabric of life. 'It is the presupposed in all human relationships.'[2] Indeed, 'the face to face is a final and irreducible relation' that 'makes possible the pluralism of society.'[3] We place a high value on interpersonal relationships as central to human life. We would be less than human if our lives were simply lost in large, anonymous structures, like 'cogs in a machine.' A question nevertheless arises: How do we understand relations that extend into the larger concerns of society – 'forms of togetherness' that are implicated in more than the immediacies of the face-to-face relation? Social existence means existence with *more than one* which brings before us questions concerned with *every one* – forms of togetherness that necessarily involve questions of politics, society, equality, just laws, and so on. In other words, how does Levinas' insistence on the singular call to responsibility – the face-to-face relation, the one-for-the-other – also address the social and political dimensions of human existence, the 'many-faced otherness'?[4]

Social Justice

The extension of love into society – into multiplicity – is what we generally call 'justice' or 'social justice.' It requires dealing with more than one, and yet Levinas insists: 'Justice, exercised through institutions, which are inevitable, must always be held in check by the initial interpersonal relation.'[5] In other words, the face-to-face relation inspires and elicits, rather than impedes, the many-faced otherness that forms the social body. 'My relation with the other as my neighbour gives meaning to my relation with all others.'[6]

Levinas' major works were written after the devastation of the Holocaust. Our ethical philosophies and social frameworks seem to have failed us terribly. Why? According to Levinas, it is because we

---

[2] Emmanuel Levinas, *Ethics and Infinity: Conversations with Philippe Nemo* (Pittsburgh: Duquesne University Press, 1985), 89.
[3] Emmanuel Levinas, *Totality and Infinity: An Essay on Exteriority* (Pittsburgh: Duquesne University Press, 1969), 291.
[4] An extended treatment of this question can be found in Terry A. Veling, *For You Alone: Emmanuel Levinas and the Answerable Life* (Eugene, Oregon: Cascade Books, 2014), Ch. 5.
[5] Levinas, *Ethics and Infinity*, 90.
[6] Emmanuel Levinas, *Otherwise Than Being or Beyond Essence* (Dordrecht: Kluwer Academic, 1991), 159.

have failed to honour the prior, fundamental, primordial ethical relation of being-for-the-other and responsibility for the other. Like a red-hot iron, Levinas purposefully intensifies and burns into our thinking the central ethical import of the face-to-face relation as that which lies as the very source of every human endeavour, every human reflection and every human encounter. 'A state in which the interpersonal relationship is impossible,' Levinas says, 'is a totalitarian state.'[7]

Levinas worries about large systems that seek to organise human communities into 'collective unities.' He is concerned that the unique, singular human being is lost or 'smothered' by large social systems and structures. He is suspicious of words such as 'unity,' 'oneness,' 'sameness.' The quest for common identities can create those who are 'in' and those who are 'out,' leading to exclusionary and excommunicative practices. Even the phrase, 'unity in diversity' *(E pluribus unum)*, while a noble sentiment, can nevertheless suggest that strangeness, difference, and diversity are welcomed and celebrated – but only if there is 'unity' – as though there were a secret fear that the stranger might actually disrupt or threaten the gathering-together of a community or a society or a nation. Welcome is extended, but only insofar as unity is preserved and not threatened. Perhaps this is why immigration policy is always such a controversial subject, because people fear the breakdown of society. We tend to prefer unified and harmonious worlds of peace and oneness, which is not always good news for the alien or for the one who doesn't fit.

Added to this, there is a danger that social systems and institutions become *self-serving*, rather than serving the people they were created for. 'The Sabbath (law/system/institution) was made for humankind, not humankind for the Sabbath' (see Mark 2:27). Universities are made for students, governments for people, hospitals for the sick, and so on. Yet sometimes institutions lose their way and need to be called again to their initial vocation, which is why institutions are especially in need of constant reform, lest they become stale and ossified. 'The charity of one-for-the-Other is never completely fulfilled by public justice or any socio-political system. This is why justice has constant need of review, reform and renewal.'[8]

---

[7] Emmanuel Levinas, *Entre Nous: Thinking-of-the-Other* (New York: Columbia University Press, 1998), 105.

[8] Roger Burggraeve, *The Wisdom of Love in the Service of Love: Emmanuel Levinas on Justice, Peace, and Human Rights* (Milwaukee: Marquette University Press, 2002), 148, 150.

Levinas does not ignore the questions and concerns of politics and social existence. His insistence on the face-to-face relation is not an apolitical stance; rather, it is the very prompting of a transformed conception of politics and society, one that keeps before us the face of the human other who is irreducible to any form of totalising politics. 'The social relation engenders the surplus of the Good over being, multiplicity over the One.'[9]

Levinas is suspicious of philosophical systems that strive for all-encompassing frameworks, blankets of thought that are large enough to cover it all. Into this blanketing system he introduces the 'other' – who escapes, refuses, transcends, interrupts, exposes, questions the system (the 'same'). Levinas brings the singular, vulnerable face of the other as witness and judge against the all-powerful system. In this sense, the other is 'outside' the system as exteriority and transcendence. He writes:

> The history of modern Europe attests to an obsession with an order to be established on universal but abstract rules – i.e. political rules, while underestimating or forgetting the uniqueness of the other person, whose right is, after all, at the origin of rights, yet always a new calling. The history of modern Europe is the permanent temptation of an ideological rationalism, and of experiments carried out through the rigor of deduction, administration and violence. A philosophy of history, a dialectic leading to peace among men – is such a thing possible after the Gulag and Auschwitz?[10]

'Politics left to itself,' writes Levinas, 'bears a tyranny within itself; it deforms the I and the other who have given rise to it, for it judges them according to universal rules, and thus *in absentia*.'[11] The workings and determinations of justice are often conducted in the great halls of the law, in the manner of a 'politics left to itself' and its own devices, as though politics had no other concern than its own concern, whereas all the time it should be concerned with the well-being of the *polis* and the common good. And all too often, rules and legislation and judgments

---
[9] Levinas, *Totality and Infinity, In the Time of the Nations* (London: Continuum, 2007), 292.
[10] Levinas, (2007), *Totality and Infinity*, 121.
[11] Levinas, (2007), *Totality and Infinity*, 300.

are made in the absence of the one who stands outside – 'in absentia' – as though the law didn't really care about those left standing outside its gates, whereas all the time it is meant to be concerned for the welfare of all, even and especially for the least of all.

Left to itself, the wheels of politics and the laws of justice can turn with unrelenting power – 'oh, the violence of administration!' Levinas cries.[12] The processes and systems of management are everywhere in our lives. Knowingly or unknowingly, we are entangled in procedures of power, policy and paperwork. Hannah Arendt calls it our 'infinitely complex red-tape existence.'[13] 'Every attempt to organise humanity fails,' writes Levinas.[14]

Administration is meant to serve the smooth running of things, in an orderly fashion. Yet too often, administration becomes a labyrinth of policy and regulation, governed by heads of departments, and before you know it, everyone is under the governance of administrators. Administrators frame everything according to the justice of the system. If there is anyone who may have a more lenient or compassionate heart, if there is anyone who may have a creative vision, if there is anyone who deviates, then these people will never become administrators. The institution will ensure this. The institution weeds out the weak ones and rewards those who ensure the strength of the system. Administrators become masters who seem strangely unaware of their servitude to the system. They forget the origin of the word 'administration' – ministratio – to serve and to heal, to administer medications and remedies, to help heal the sick and aid those in need. Pope Paul VI writes: 'If beyond legal rules, there is no deeper feeling of respect for and service to others, then even equality before the law can serve as an alibi for fragrant discrimination, continued exploitation, and actual contempt.'[15]

---

[12] Emmanuel Levinas, *Is It Righteous to Be? Interviews with Emmanuel Levinas* (Stanford: Stanford University Press, 2001), 51.
[13] Hannah Arendt, *The Portable Hannah Arendt* (New York: Penguin, 2000), 25.
[14] Levinas, (2001), *Is It Righteous to Be?* 217.
[15] Pope Paul VI, *Octogesima Adveniens: A Call to Action*, no. 23. Retrieved from www.vatican.va.

Certain strains of Catholic social teaching express a suspicion toward grandiose and yet vain political programs. In his encyclical, 'A Call to Action,' for example, Pope Paul VI worries about the ambiguity inherent in every social ideology. Sometimes it leads political or social activity to be simply the application of an abstract, purely theoretical idea . . . There is also the danger of giving adherence to an ideology which does not rest on a true and organic doctrine, to take refuge in it as a final and sufficient explanation of everything, and thus to build a new idol, accepting, at times without being aware of doing so, its totalitarian and coercive character. And people imagine they find in it a justification for their activity, even violent activity, and an adequate response to a desire to serve. The desire remains but it allows itself to be consumed by an ideology which, even if it suggests certain paths to man's liberation, ends up by making him a slave.[16]

Like Levinas, Paul VI worries that 'politics left to itself' holds the inherent danger, even under the banner of a desire to serve, of turning the law and politics into an idol. Even democracy can be turned into an idol as, for example, the way it is often invoked by those who seek a justification for the 'war on terror.' Violence can spread even in the name of democracy and freedom, especially if these are taken as 'a final and sufficient explanation of everything.' Paul VI offers the following caution: 'Politics are a demanding manner – but not the only one – of living the Christian commitment to service to others . . . The domain of politics is wide and comprehensive, but it is not exclusive. An attitude of encroachment which would tend to set up politics as an absolute value would bring serious danger.'[17]

Our social institutions, political administrations, judicial systems are not so much the basis or *foundation* of ethical relations, but the *consequence* or *guardianship* of the more primary ethical relation that comes to us, not from our well-constructed ethical codes or social systems, but from the fundamental relationship of the 'I and the other.' If our social and political frameworks are not directed toward or inspired by this fundamental ethical relationship, they are in danger of forgetting real faces and real speech and becoming tyrannies.

---

[16] Pope Paul VI, *Octogesima Adveniens: A Call to Action,* nos. 27-28.
[17] Paul VI, *Octogesima Adveniens: A Call to Action,* no. 46.

Levinas thinks it defies logic – or even a basic sense of humanity – to attempt to compare the incomparable. The human person is 'an absolute identity – non-interchangeable, incomparable and unique.'[18] He cites a Talmudic metaphor concerning the minting of coins: 'Behold man, who strikes all coins with the same die and gets coins all alike; but behold the Holy-Blessed-Be-He, who strikes all men with the die of Adam and not one is the same as another.'[19] Human beings are not like minted coins, interchangeable and alike; rather, human beings are incomparable and unique, made in the image of God.

Nevertheless, Levinas recognises that comparison is inevitable. 'Must not human beings, who are incomparable, be compared?'[20] He acknowledges that there is a certain 'necessity of thinking together under a synthetic theme the multiplicity and the unity of the world.'[21] Justice 'calls for judgment and comparison, a comparison of what is in principle incomparable, for every being is unique, every other is unique.'[22] However, he insists that this Greek wisdom of ordering, must become more than philosophy's love of wisdom, but also the very biblical 'wisdom of love at the service of love.'[23] He suggests that peace can only be found in the *surplus* of the 'one' – that is, not an all-embracing 'Oneness' that gathers into a totality; rather, the *singular one* that *exceeds* these assimilating efforts.

Social Mercy

Justice implies 'giving everyone their due.' However, Jewish and Christian faith also speaks of justice *with mercy, with compassion.* God is not simply a blindfolded judge balancing the scales of justice, but is also a tender, loving, compassionate mother. Compassion and mercy are related to the Hebrew word for womb, *'rahamim.'* Maybe there is a role for equivalence and measurement in the realm of justice ('to give each his or her due'), but in the realm of love this 'logic of equivalence' gives way to a 'poetics of love' or what Paul Ricoeur calls

---

[18] Emmanuel Levinas, *Outside the Subject* (Stanford: Stanford University Press, 1993), 117.
[19] Levinas, (1993), *Outside the Subject,* 118.
[20] Levinas, *Entre Nous,* 104.
[21] Emmanuel Levinas, *Basic Philosophical Writings* (Bloomington: Indiana University Press, 1996), 168.
[22] Levinas, *Entre Nous,* 104.
[23] Levinas, *Basic Philosophical Writings,* 169.

the 'logic of superabundance.'[24] Superabundant love is excessive and immeasurable. It is 'crazy love' that gives without counting, or seeking for a just equivalence.

Along with Ricoeur, Levinas was regularly invited to Saint Pope John Paul II's summer residence on the outskirts of Rome. John Paul II saw Levinas as 'the model of a great Jewish thinker.'[25] Similarly, Levinas had a great respect for the pope's religious vision. John Paul II was insistent that justice alone cannot save us, but requires the merciful love of God's compassion. Levinas is in accord: 'Justice itself is born of charity,' he writes.[26] 'We should never forget that justice comes from *chesed* – favour, goodness, loving-kindness.'[27]

There is much that is unjust in our society, yet I have wondered whether it is the lack of mercy that causes injustice to prevail. Or rather, that without mercy, justice is perilously close to becoming unjust. Mercy is not the opposite of justice – or the complement of justice – but its very condition. What sort of statements would we make, or what type of policies would we devise, or what kind of actions would we promote, if we were to speak of 'social mercy' as resolutely as we speak of 'social justice'?[28]

In his encyclical, 'Rich in Mercy,' John Paul II suggests that justice can become an idol: 'Human action can deviate from justice itself, even when it is being undertaken in the name of justice.'[29] We can easily deceive ourselves into thinking that we are acting justly and, for this reason, Pope John Paul II suggests that without mercy, justice cannot be established. 'The experience of the past and of our own time demonstrates that justice alone is not enough, that it can even lead to the negation of itself, if that deeper power, which is love, is not allowed to shape human life in its various dimensions.'[30] The pope goes on to

---

[24] Paul Ricoeur, *Figuring the Sacred: Religion, Narrative and Imagination* (Minneapolis: Fortress Press, 1995), 329.
[25] Salomon Malka, *Emmanuel Levinas: His Life and Legacy* (Pittsburgh: Duquesne University Press, 2006), 209.
[26] Levinas, (2001), *Is It Righteous to Be?* 168.
[27] Emmanuel Levinas, 'Interview with Emmanuel Levinas,' Edith Wyschogrod. *Philosophy and Theology* 4 (1989), 106.
[28] Terry A. Veling, *The Beatitude of Mercy: Love Watches Over Justice* (Eugene, Oregon: Wipf and Stock Publishers, 2015).
[29] Pope John Paul II, *Dives in Misericordia: On the Mercy of God* (Homebush, NSW: St Paul Publications, 1980), 58.
[30] Pope John Paul II, *Dives in Misericordia*, 58-59.

say: *'Mercy differs from justice but is not in opposition to it.'* Rather, 'mercy conditions justice' in the sense that *'true mercy is the most profound source of justice'* and is 'a mark of the whole of revelation.'[31] In other words, mercy is not bad news for justice, but good news. 'Mercy is indispensable for shaping mutual relationships between people. It is impossible to establish this bond between people if they regulate their mutual relationships solely according to the measure of justice. In every sphere of interpersonal relationships justice must be *'corrected'* by that *merciful love* which is the essence of the Gospel and Christianity.'[32]

The seemingly fragile acts of tenderness and love – acts of social mercy – should not be considered as mere 'band-aids.' Rather, they are the very sign of God's goodness in the world. A rabbinic parable speaks of the Messiah who is found at the city gates, attending to the afflicted and the suffering, 'binding up their wounds,' and says that while 'others bind an *entire* area covering *several* wounds with one bandage, the Messiah dresses each *wound separately.*'[33]

Mercy does not diminish human value and dignity; rather, it acts to restore the dignity that is proper to human life. According to Pope John Paul II, 'Mercy is manifested in its true and proper aspect when it restores to value, promotes and *draws good from all the forms of evil* existing in the world and in the person.'[34]

The Constitution of Society

The works of Emmanuel Levinas are remarkable in the constancy of their thought and the strength of their appeal – we are here on this spinning blue planet not by any chance, but by a bond that urges us to be one-for-the-other, to carry each other, to be for each other, to escape the narrow confines of our small egoism. Beyond the realms of the academy, Levinas bears an important message for us to hear, even given the complexities of his thinking. No matter where I have lived – Sydney, Boston, Jerusalem, Miami, Brisbane – one thing strikes me as

---

[31] Pope John Paul II, *Dives in Misericordia*, 26, 68.
[32] Pope John Paul II, *Dives in Misericordia*, 69.
[33] Chaim Pearl, *Theology in Rabbinic Stories* (Peabody, MA: Hendrickson, 1997), 145 (citing *Sanhedrin* 98a).
[34] Pope John Paul II, *Dives in Misericordia*, 36.

constant – the lives of ordinary people. I don't share the same burdens of the poor and the afflicted; I'm simply one among many who ride the buses every day. And I think to myself, there must be a way of helping us turn toward each other. Yet I doubt this will be possible unless we learn again what it means to undergo a 'conversion of heart' – a *metanoia* – a way of turning around to face the other – in our very midst, yet only so because always beyond ourselves. According to Levinas, this turning toward, this face-to-face, is the essential divine and ethical relation:

> Perhaps the spiritual only shows, only reveals its specificity when being's routine is interrupted: in the strangeness of humans vis-à-vis one another, but of humans capable of a sociality in which the bond is no longer the integration of parts in a whole. Perhaps the spiritual bond lies in the non-indifference of persons toward one another that is also called love, but that does not absorb the difference and strangeness and is possible only on the basis of a spoken word or order coming, through the human face, from most high outside the world.[35]

What constitutes society? Levinas insists that it is the interpersonal and face-to-face relation that ultimately constitutes society. When speaking to Christian audiences, he often referred to chapter 25 of Matthew's Gospel: 'in so far as you did this to one of the least . . .' He writes: 'The relation to God is presented there as a relation to another human person. It is not a metaphor; in the other, there is a real presence of God. In my relation to the other, I hear the word of God. It is not a metaphor. It is not only extremely important; it is literally true. I'm not saying that the other is God, but that in his or her face I hear the word of God.'[36]

In similar fashion, one of the cardinal points of Catholic social teaching is that the human person 'is the foundation, the cause and the end of every social institution.'[37] The reference is not to the human person as an *individual*, but the human person who is in relation with other persons and with all that is alive and living in God's good

---

[35] Levinas, (1993), *Outside the Subject*, 102-3.
[36] Levinas, (2001), *Is It Righteous to Be?* 171.
[37] Pope John XXIII, *Mater et Magistra: Christianity and Social Progress*, 219. www.vatican.va. Accessed 31 July 2016.

creation. Some may wonder whether Levinas' constitution of society is simply a utopian or high-minded ideal. When Levinas was asked whether his thought was utopian and unrealistic, he replied:

> This is the great objection to my thought. 'Where did you ever see the ethical relation practiced?' people say to me. I reply that its being utopian does not prevent it from investing our everyday actions with generosity and goodwill towards the other... This concern for the other remains utopian in the sense that it is always 'out of place *(u-topos)* in this world, always other than the 'ways of the world': but there are many examples of it in the world.[38]

Dorothy Day's Catholic Worker Houses are perhaps one example of this, along with her typewriter in which she constantly advocated for the poor and disadvantaged. She writes: 'God made heaven hinge on the way we act toward him in his disguise of commonplace, frail, ordinary humanity.'[39] Levinas writes in a similar vein:

> I am thinking of a God whose grandeur, whose justice and mercy *(rachamim)* you see everywhere. It is Christian too. I do not say it is uniquely Jewish. You see God's humility; it is a God who comes down, who has not negated the finite but has entered into the finite. This means it is a God who has sent you the other human being. This is the constitution of society: there is a human being sent toward the other human being. This is my central thesis and consequently it is this structure that is divinity.[40]

According to Levinas, it is not violence or hatred that is the original condition of life; rather, it is the ethical relation of being-for-the-other. While violence persists, it always fails or always persists as failure. What outlasts violence, what is always more 'victorious,' is a love without measure, an infinite love that is stronger than death,

---

[38] Emmanuel Levinas, "Dialogue with Emmanuel Levinas." Emmanuel Levinas and Richard Kearney. In *Face to Face with Levinas,* edited by Richard A. Cohen (Albany: State University of New York Press, 1986), 32.

[39] Cited in Paul Elie, *The Life You Save May Be Your Own: An American Pilgrimage* (New York: Farrar, Straus and Giroux, 2003), 225.

[40] Levinas, (1989), 'Interview with Emmanuel Levinas', 107.

a love that proves the futility and ultimate failure of violence. 'This infinity, stronger than murder, already resists in his face, is his face, is the primordial *expression*, is the first word: "you shall not commit murder".'[41] The original relation is peace, non-violence, the biblical kingdom of love – a kingdom that 'paralyses power' by its 'infinite resistance' to murder and hatred.[42] Love, which 'gleams in the face of the Other,' cannot be killed – and all those who have died at the hands of human hatred are both judge and witness to this.

The biblical command to 'love your neighbour' is not a realm of knowledge beyond our reach, but a teaching that teaches us what is possible. Rabbi Tarfon says: 'You are not required to complete the task, yet neither are you free to withdraw from it.'[43]

---

[41] Levinas, (2007), *Totality and Infinity*, 199.
[42] Levinas, (2007), *Totality and Infinity*, 199.
[43] *Pirkei Avos, Ethics of the Fathers* (New York: Mesorah Press, 1989), 2:21.

Chapter Seven

The Emerging Approach to Political Economy of Pope Francis

Brendan Long

Five years into the pontificate of Pope Francis, many different themes of his theological leadership are emerging. His engagement with the economic world is a key early theme. The task here is to track his progress on this issue and draw from it some lessons that can be applied to the Australian context.

Pope Francis has already demonstrated in his theological and pastoral statements a key interest in what can be called political economy. This universe of discourse is much more easily referred to than defined. There are starkly different perspectives in play and all of these have their representatives in the Roman Catholic intellectual world. There is a more socialist element on the left of the political spectrum aligned with the thought of liberation theologians who seem to call for a revolutionary challenge to the modern capitalist world.

Political economy for them is liberation from economic oppression seen as being embodied in current international economic dynamics and the international financial institutions that form part of this global process. This genre of Catholic voices might see Francis as an ally in their cause. On the other side of the spectrum we have liberal minds who critique contemporary economic structures from a broad perspective of the political right, aligned with political liberalism, which is enjoying a new renaissance in the United States. For those of this perspective, political economy tends to emphasise how the rights of individuals are hindered by an overreaching state. They appeal to elements of Catholic social thought that support this view based on a strong reading of the principle of subsidiarity. Pope Francis himself was personally drawn into this ebullient cauldron in the 2016 US

Republican Presidential Primary process, when he was embroiled into a debate with Donald Trump over immigration issues in February 2016.

First, we must accept that Francis' views on political economy are emerging and the emergence is a function of the way the man operates personally. His method contrasts to the approach taken by his immediate predecessors. Pope St John Paul II wrote sophisticated works of theology and philosophy seeking to engage the economic world with influence. Benedict XVI focused on creating a theological discussion between faith and reason. Francis seems to prefer to focus on a praxis of engagement which emphasises a pastoral and deeply spiritual connection with all people, especially those who are marginalised. His method of dialogue is fresh, effusive and warm. By personality, and probably by virtue of his Latino temperament, he tends to like to speak freely from the heart. So it is important to weigh his thoughts, and seek central themes rather than to focus on a particular statement in isolation, written or spoken. However, Francis has entered this debate with some force. There can be no doubt that he presents a kerygmatic challenge and call for metanoia to the economic community.

Reflective Praxis

As Terry Veling attests, practical theology is not just simply an exercise in applying religious insights to real world problems but reflecting on how theological thinking infuses the way we approach practical concerns.[1] It is a reflective praxis. This method captures Francis' approach to political economy. This reflective praxis is seen in Francis' engagement with the international community with a renewed vision of how the Catholic Church approaches the key social policy challenges of global inequality and climate change.

Francis' reflective praxis is innovative in two ways. The first is essentially political and the second is deeply spiritual, but both elements are mutually reinforcing. In *Evangelii Gaudium* we see a discursive reflection on social concerns critical of the role of international market-based forces and speaking for compassionate approaches: an epistle

---

[1] Terry A. Veling, *Practical theology: on Earth as it is in heaven*, (Orbis: Maryknoll, 2005).

that seriously engages the problem of social inequality. In *Laudato Si'* we have a strong statement of the need for commitment to action on climate change but also a document that critiques consumerist elements of modern life: the 'throw away' culture in society. This is a strong call for social engagement from a left of centre political perspective combining environment concerns with an appreciation of the need to combat poverty and a degraded economic order.

Evangelii Gaudium

Pope Francis' first engagement on the question of economics is found in the Apostolic Exhortation *Evangelii Gaudium*. True to its title, it is a wide-ranging statement of a joyful and praise-filled vision of Christ's word of love for all. However, strong criticisms are made especially in the economic area. In fact, Francis' language on the influence of economic forces on marginalised persons, the poor, is strident and confronting, especially for the professional economist and practical theologian who engages with economics.

In *Evangelii Gaudium*, Francis emphasises how global economic forces exacerbate the problem of social exclusion. In using this language, Francis is identifying himself with a movement in social enquiry which looks beyond purely measured outcomes of inequity but adopts a wider view of economic disadvantage that examines how the capacity of an individual to achieve his/her natural abilities is restricted, with consequent implications for their capacity to participate in the wider community. We can take Amartya Sen's insightful work on 'Development as Freedom' as a strong statement of this viewpoint from an economic perspective.[2] Francis' call is made clear in a section heading in *Evangelii Gaudium* titled 'No to an economy of exclusion'. His message is that poverty is not just the result of a form of social exploitation or oppression which would flow from a typical Marxist perspective. His challenge is different. It is not social structures or class mechanisms that drive social exclusion, but an instinct in the human person him/herself to see themselves solely as consumers and ultimately to see other persons as consumer goods.

---

[2] Amartya Sen, *Development as Freedom* (Oxford University Press: New York, 1999).

Just as the commandment 'Thou shalt not kill' sets a clear limit in order to safeguard the value of human life, today we also have to say 'thou shalt not' to an economy of exclusion and inequality. Such an economy kills... Human beings are themselves considered consumer goods to be used and then discarded. We have created a 'throw away' culture which is now spreading. It is no longer simply about exploitation and oppression, but something new. (EG,53).

Who is being killed by the consumer culture that throws away things? It is living human beings who are killed – we kill others by treating them as mere objects of consumption in our participation in an economic system which makes people merely goods that can be discarded. It is very strong language, rather than honed prose of the typical papal Apostolic Exhortation! Let us seek to analyse this dual lens of the theological and the economist.

Starting with the theological lens, we can note that what Francis is appealing to is not a claim that we directly decide to harm, least of all kill, others by deciding individually to treat other persons as means to our personal ends. This would reduce all of us to monsters. Rather, it seems, he invokes the long tradition in Christian theological reflection, and represented in the views of Augustine, that we must see persons as the ultimate ends of our social engagement, not as means to our own ends.[3] We can be implicated in economic engagement unconsciously which embodies a process which can be evil in that it leads to a degradation of others' dignity through complex and unforeseen economic processes. Francis' view could be seen as an application of the notion of original sin to economics. In Catholic theology, original sin is not sin as understood as bad acts. Original sin is only analogous to the notion of sin as evil choices. Through original sin, we are thrown into a broken world prior to our choice and which we cannot escape without some sense of participation.[4]

---

[3] Karl Rahner, 'The Sin of Adam', *Theological Investigations*, Volume 11, (London: Darton, Longman and Todd, 1963), 247-262. See also John D. Mueller, *Redeeming Economics: Rediscovering the Missing Element*, (Wilmington: ISI Books, 2010).
[4] I have sought to explore this notion of original sin in economics, see for example Brendan Long, 'Adam Smith's Theodicy', Paul Oslington (Editor), *Adam Smith as Theologian*, (New York: Routledge, 2011).

If such economic participation seems to create evil in the world, by treating persons as means in a consumerist society rather than ends, the Gospel message is still a *metanoia*, a call to repentance even if the choice is not one of personal sin but of social participation in a process with evil consequences. The response of the Christian is hope for redemption of all things in the reconciling action of God's incarnate love in Christ. Still, the passionate nature of this language from the Pope seems to have something of a shock effect – to call us to look for evil in our everyday economic lives. For Francis, we seem to be inoculated or anaesthetised against realising this, so addicted have we become to the allure of the consumerist society.

Francis' language brings a passionate directness to the challenges he presents. However, his views continue the lines of criticism developed by Pope St Paul John II and Benedict XVI, who in turn sought to develop the corpus of Catholic social thought beginning with *Rerum Novarum* of Leo XIII. Francis' views align with the statements of Pope St John Paul II in his seminal encyclical– *Laborem Exercens* – which rejects materialistic approaches to economic thought.

In the modern period, from the beginning of the industrial age, the Christian truth about work had to oppose the various trends of materialistic and economistic thought. (LE, 7).

Benedict XVI was highly critical of the excesses of the economic order and called for an ethical approach to economics that recognises the moral needs of persons. In his encyclical *Caritas in Veritate*, which includes a substantive response to the global economic crisis of this period, he emphasis that the 'logic of gift' requires economics to be based on moral concerns.[5]

> ... the conviction that the economy must be autonomous, that it must be shielded from 'influences' of a moral character, has led man to abuse the economic process in a thoroughly destructive way. In the long term, these convictions have led to economic, social and political systems that trample upon personal and social freedom, and are therefore unable to deliver the justice that they promise. (CV, 34).

---

[5] See Brendan Long, 'Political Implications of Caritas in Veritate', Neil Ormerod and Paul Oslington (Editors), *Globalisation and the Church: reflections on Caritas in Veritate*, (St Pauls Publications: Strathfield, 2011).

> Striving to meet the deepest moral needs of the person also has important and beneficial repercussions at the level of economics. The economy needs ethics in order to function correctly — not any ethics whatsoever, but an ethics which is people-centred. (CV. 45).

Francis' is highly critical in *Evangelii Gaudium* of a market-based ideology. Francis clearly rejects the general approach of economic discourse, founded in Adam Smith's famous notion of the 'invisible hand', which claims that, in the aggregate, individual pursuit of self-love through a free market usually leads to higher social welfare. Francis offers a cultural critique of this methodological individualism, a stated credo of contemporary economic discourse. He believes that this culture of personal and collective prosperity erodes us from within spiritually as we succumb to the delusive allure of personal consumption. He claims that such a methodology of economic thinking fails to deliver on its alluring promise of greater good for the whole community. He reduces this process to a paltry trickle-down effect which does not deliver justice and creates social exclusion.

> In this context, some people continue to defend trickle-down theories which assume that economic growth, encouraged by a free market, will inevitably succeed in bringing about greater justice and inclusiveness in the world... The culture of prosperity deadens us; we are thrilled if the market offers us something new to purchase (EG, 54).

Francis says in another section heading in the document 'No to the new idolatry of money'. His claim is clear. The hegemony of economic institutions in our everyday economic life, labeled as having an 'absolute autonomy', leads to financial speculation which exacerbates economic inequality. Here he is reflecting on the actual impact of the global financial crisis.

> While the earnings of a minority are growing exponentially, so too is the gap separating the majority from the prosperity enjoyed by those happy few. This imbalance is the result of ideologies which defend the absolute autonomy of the marketplace and financial speculation (EG, 56)

His claim is clear. The hegemony of economic institutions in our everyday economic life – seen as having an 'absolute autonomy'– leads to financial speculation which exacerbates economic inequality. Here he is soberly reflecting on the actual impact of the global financial crisis.

In short, in *Evangelii Gaudium*, Pope Francis presents a theological critique of contemporary capitalism. It is an epistle from the political left in strident terms reflecting his experience as a pastor in Argentina. His country defaulted on its national debt in 2001, causing extreme hardship for individuals who had to deal with hyperinflation where the price of bread can rise significantly between sunrise and sunset, leading to Argentina being locked out of international financial markets for fifteen years. It is easy to track the origin of Francis' passion in this matter.

While the suffering of the people of Argentina as a result of the action of global financial institutions is manifest over a sustained period, the claim can be made that these outcomes flow from imprudent fiscal management by the Argentine Government.[6] Moreover, the adverse effects of the global financial crisis relate to failures of US Government officials to properly regulate the financial institutions within their jurisdiction. Indeed, some of Francis' attack on contemporary economic thinking may in fact reflect more of a failure of prudent regulatory management of economic activity rather than the activity itself. However, Francis makes a stronger claim. He is not just saying that the economy has failed so many but why it continues to foster injustice and exclusion. He offers the challenge that the ultimate reason for social exclusion through economic media lies in our own hearts. Deadened by a culture of consumerism, we allow the 'absolute autonomy' of economic processes to proceed on their headlong course because we who have wealth are addicted to the trinkets of our personal consumption (the latest I-phone, the new car or, in Australia, the great housing upgrade).

In effect, Francis is challenging the theoretical foundations of contemporary economic philosophy and labelling them as immoral –

---

[6] See Brenden Long, Neil Ormerod & Paul Oslington, (Editors) *Globalisation and the Church: Reflections On Caritas In Veritate*, (2011), 135-148.

as a culture that kills. He calls for a cultural renewal of the fundamental precepts that ground our economic life.

Laudato Si'

If we can take an analogy from cricket, as we Australians are at times prone to, in Francis' first over against the economic World XI, in *Evangelii Gaudium*, Francis bowled fast and short. However, the truth is that he was only warming up. In *Laudato Si'* - his first encyclical – he finds line and length. If in *Evangelii Gaudium* there is a passionate presentation of the social costs of the exuberance of economic forces seen in the global financial crisis, in *Laudato Si'* we see an emerging new approach to the relationship between Christian theology and central social and economic issues. *Laudato Si'* is highly critical in tone and content of contemporary economic institutions, but is also supported by a strong positive message of the power of Christian spirituality to open a new way of approaching the complex discussion between theology and economics. This way appears to be an appeal to an economic asceticism that should be adopted for the sake of the common good. It is neither a morose nor dour asceticism, but at once a joyous movement that finds liberation through the enhancement of the common good in the praise of God's gift of creation.

The topic of *Laudato Si'* is climate change. Francis not only accepts that climate change is a strong moral challenge, but he aligns this concern with his views on social exclusion. Climate change is hurting the poor.

> I will point to the intimate relationship between the poor and the fragility of the planet, the conviction that everything in the world is connected, the critique of new paradigms and forms of power derived from technology, the call to seek other ways of understanding the economy and progress, the value proper to each creature, the human meaning of ecology ... (LS, 16)

The central notion of Catholic social teaching is the notion of the common good. Francis, working with the traditional definition of the common good in Catholic social teaching, sees the climate itself as a common good.

> An integral ecology is inseparable from the notion of the common good, a central and unifying principle of social ethics. The common good is 'the sum of those conditions of social life which allow social groups and their individual members relatively thorough and ready access to their own fulfillment' (LS, 156).
>
> The climate is a common good, belonging to all and meant for all. At the global level, it is a complex system linked to many of the essential conditions for human life. A very solid scientific consensus indicates that we are presently witnessing a disturbing warming of the climatic system. In recent decades, this warming has been accompanied by a constant rise in the sea level and, it would appear, by an increase of extreme weather events, even if a scientifically determinable cause cannot be assigned to each particular phenomenon. Humanity is called to recognise the need for changes of lifestyle, production and consumption, in order to combat this warming or at least the human causes which produce or aggravate it (LS, 23).

Francis makes two points here. Climate change is definitely real. The second point is that it is a function of economic decisions of 'lifestyle, production and consumption' which either 'produce it or aggravate it'. There is a clear 'no' here to any climate change scepticism. He calls for drastic reduction in emissions which are the result of consumption and productions decisions.

> Many of those who possess more resources and economic or political power seem mostly to be concerned with masking the problems or concealing their symptoms, simply making efforts to reduce some of the negative impacts of climate change. However, many of these symptoms indicate that such effects will continue to worsen if we continue with current models of production and consumption. There is an urgent need to develop policies so that, in the next few years, the emission of carbon dioxide and other highly polluting gases can be drastically reduced, for example, substituting for fossil fuels and developing sources of renewable energy (LS, 26).

His position is extended further. He does not see that the solution to the erosion of the common good of our climate is adequately met by even the strong policy measures of carbon trading taken by previous Australian governments or the EU model.

> The strategy of buying and selling 'carbon credits' can lead to a new form of speculation which would not help reduce the emission of polluting gases worldwide (LS, 171).

Francis explicitly links adverse climate change to social exclusion. He sees it as part of a general approach to technological innovation which builds social disadvantage in myriad forms reducing social cohesion.

> The social dimensions of global change include the effects of technological innovation on employment, social exclusion, an inequitable distribution and consumption of energy and other services, social breakdown, increased violence and a rise in new forms of social aggression, drug trafficking, growing drug use by young people, and the loss of identity. These are signs that the growth of the past two centuries has not always led to an integral development and an improvement in the quality of life. Some of these signs are also symptomatic of real social decline, the silent rupture of the bonds of integration and social cohesion (LS, 46).

Francis' key theme is to link the social effects of climate change with the North/South frontier of economic exclusion (a classic South American form of rhetoric) evoking the notion of ecological debt with the economic indebtedness of South American countries and other developing countries.

> Inequity affects not only individuals but entire countries; it compels us to consider an ethics of international relations. A true 'ecological debt' exists, particularly between the global north and south, connected to commercial imbalances with effects on the environment, and the disproportionate use of natural resources by certain countries over long periods of time (LS, 51).

Here we see a clear theme of the encyclical. Francis is deeply troubled by the pervasive effects of international indebtedness of poorer countries, reflecting again his experience as a pastor in Argentina. Whereas the poor 'South' owes money to the rich 'North', through the developed world's greater impact on climate change it owes an 'ecological debt' to poorer countries. So the developed world should pay for its ecological debt to the less developed countries if they have to pay their economic debt to richer ones.

However, there is a structural perversity in economic relations. The rich countries consumption leads to patterns of ownership which don't fuel social development needs in poor countries. Rich countries should take policies to fuel economic development of poor countries in recognition of the ecological debt they owe to the world. Francis says that they fail to do this. He seems to suggest that if the developed world owes an ecological debt to the whole world, it should at least recognise this when it seeks to further impoverish the developing world to pay its financial debts to the developed world.

> The foreign debt of poor countries has become a way of controlling them, yet this is not the case where ecological debt is concerned. In different ways, developing countries, where the most important reserves of the biosphere are found, continue to fuel the development of richer countries at the cost of their own present and future. The land of the southern poor is rich and mostly unpolluted, yet access to ownership of goods and resources for meeting vital needs is inhibited by a system of commercial relations and ownership which is structurally perverse. The developed countries ought to help pay this debt by significantly limiting their consumption of non-renewable energy and by assisting poorer countries to support policies and programmes of sustainable development (LS, 52).

Economic asceticism

For Francis, the ecological problem and the problem of economic disadvantage are united. In fact, Francis appears to use the environmental problem of climate change in *Laudato Si'* to develop his concerns about how economic inequality is structurally integrated into the international economy presented in *Evangelii Gaudium*. The ecological problem highlights and exacerbates the inequality problem. The problem is that we still lack the culture needed to confront this crisis' (LS, 53). 'It is remarkable how weak international political responses have been' (LS, 54).

> In the meantime, economic powers continue to justify the current global system where priority tends to be given to speculation and the pursuit of financial gain, which fail to take the context into account, let alone the effects on human dignity and the natural environment. Here we see how environmental deterioration and human and ethical degradation are closely linked (LS, 56).

Francis is also critical of the role technology has played in undermining the common good in ecological matters and in fighting social inequality.

> Humanity has entered a new era in which our technical prowess has brought us to a crossroads (LS, 102).

> But human beings are not completely autonomous. Our freedom fades when it is handed over to the blind forces of the unconscious, of immediate needs, of self-interest, and of violence. In this sense, we stand naked and exposed in the face of our ever-increasing power, lacking the wherewithal to control it. We have certain superficial mechanisms, but we cannot claim to have a sound ethics, a culture and spirituality genuinely capable of setting limits and teaching clear-minded self-restraint (LS, 105).

> The technocratic paradigm also tends to dominate economic and political life. The economy accepts every advance in technology with a view to profit, without concern for its potentially negative impact on human beings. Finance overwhelms the real economy. The lessons of the global financial crisis have not been assimilated, and we are learning all too slowly the lessons of environmental deterioration (LS, 109).

A purely economic response to climate change or inequality is also implicated for Francis in cultural relativism.

> The culture of relativism is the same disorder which drives one person to take advantage of another... It is also the mindset of those who say: Let us allow the invisible forces of the market to regulate the economy, and consider their impact on society and nature as collateral damage (LS, 123).

In *Laudato Si'* like *Evangelii Gaudium* Francis does not just engage in polemic discourse but offers a way forward. What he is seeking is for political forces to offer a new alternative to the current economic paradigm with its reliance of a flawed allegiance to the teleological view that the outcome determines what is considered just and ethical.

> Politics must not be subject to the economy, nor should the economy be subject to the dictates of an efficiency-driven paradigm of technocracy... Production is not always rational, and is usually tied to economic variables which assign to products a value that does not necessarily correspond to their real worth. This frequently leads to an overproduction of some commodities, with unnecessary impact on the environment and with negative results on regional economies. The financial bubble also tends to be a productive bubble. The problem of the real economy is not confronted with vigour, yet it is the real economy which makes diversification and improvement in production possible, helps companies to function well, and enables small and medium businesses to develop and create employment (LS, 189).

> We know how unsustainable is the behaviour of those who constantly consume and destroy, while others are not yet able to live in a way worthy of their human dignity (LS,193).

> ... economics without politics cannot be justified, since this would make it impossible to favour other ways of handling the various aspects of the present crisis. The mindset which leaves no room for sincere concern for the environment is the same mindset which lacks concern for the inclusion of the most

vulnerable members of society. For 'the current model, with its emphasis on success and self-reliance, does not appear to favour an investment in efforts to help the slow, the weak or the less talented to find opportunities in life' (LS,196).

What Francis seeks is a new political economy which combats the dominate paradigm of consumption and production in market forces with a new approach which recognises that there are excesses in normal economic processes which, without government policy, will erode the common good of the climate and social inclusion. It is a radical message. He calls for a certain economic asceticism. He calls for a charitable and faith-filled response to dial back the excesses of the market economy as they lead to environmental and social evils. He wants us to give away the throw-away culture that he sees present in consumerist society and calls for a change to personal consumption habits for the sake of the common good. He says strongly that less (in terms of personal consumption) can yield a more – the common good.

> It is the conviction that 'less is more'. A constant flood of new consumer goods can baffle the heart and prevent us from cherishing each thing and each moment. To be serenely present to each reality, however small it may be, opens us to much greater horizons of understanding and personal fulfilment. Christian spirituality proposes a growth marked by moderation and the capacity to be happy with little. It is a return to that simplicity which allows us to stop and appreciate the small things, to be grateful for the opportunities which life affords us, to be spiritually detached from what we possess, and not to succumb to sadness for what we lack. This implies avoiding the dynamic of dominion and the mere accumulation of pleasures (LS, 222).

> Love, overflowing with small gestures of mutual care, is also civic and political, and it makes itself felt in every action that seeks to build a better world. Love for society and commitment to the common good are outstanding expressions of a charity which affects not only relationships between individuals

but also 'macro-relationships, social, economic and political ones'. That is why the Church set before the world the ideal of a 'civilisation of love'. Social love is the key to authentic development (LS, 231).

Drawing on the tradition of asceticism in Catholic spirituality Francis makes the call in *Laudato Si'* for an economic asceticism in personal consumption decisions and in the policies that support them at the governmental level. Francis takes the spirituality of Saint Francis to show how joy is found in renunciation. Using the environmental topic of the encyclical, he announces a call for an economic asceticism that supports progressive environmental and social policies. Less is more from the spiritual perspective in matters economic. Embodied in this call is a nascent moral theology of economics based on a spiritual theology of radical Christian asceticism. He calls us to rejoice in the material renunciation of consumption that St Francis evokes not just for the sake of a personal spiritual renewal but because such a renewal serves the common good in environmental and economic terms.

Francis calls for personal asceticism in consumption choices to reject a throw-away culture embodied in modern capitalist society. He wants us to appreciate that we the rich – yes, we Australians – cause poverty in economic and environmental matters by the way we approach the economy in our personal decisions. As noted above, it is a sort of original sin doctrine applied to economic matters. Certainly, in choices of which type of margarine we buy, or which brand of coffee we purchase, we don't cause world poverty directly. However, the consumerist sentiment which is implicated in our daily lives in the developed world has implications for the way that economics is done on a global scale.

We participate in a process, maybe a process of co-determined guilt to use the terminology of Karl Rahner which has implications for others which are harmful and which we do not intend.[7] That we do not intend them directly, does not mean that they are not real, and remain for Francis a call for personal, social and political *metanoia*, a call to repentance and a response of penitence. This penitence, this *metanoia*,

---

[7] See Karl Rahner, *Foundations of Christian Faith: An Introduction to the Idea of Christianity*, translated by William V. Dych, (New York: The Seabury Press, 1978).

is a call to refrain or restrict our participation in a throw-away market economy and to seek rather to rejoice in the joy of a certain absence of material wellbeing for the sake of the Kingdom of God – a reign of God which rejoices in God himself rather than an idolatry to things. Less is more he tells us in economic concerns and yet the strength of the language he adopts leads me to think that he makes an even stronger claim – that the more is actually less from the perspective of the common good seen in terms of environmental degradation or social inequality.

Reciprocating Subsidiarity

It is not just a message of personal spiritual renewal. Francis took this message to the floor of the most celebrated democratic institution in the world – the podium of the US House of Representatives in his extraordinary speech to the combined sitting of the US Congress and Senate. It is usual in Catholic social teaching to present the principle of solidarity as primary and the principle of subsidiarity as secondary. However, this is not what he did in this speech. He called for both but first for a reciprocating subsidiarity before evoking the principle of solidarity. Perhaps this was just clever speechwriting targeted to a particularly conservative audience. However, this notion of reciprocating subsidiarity is new language. What does it mean? It seems to be an open textured notion that potentially explodes the loose sense in which the principle of subsidiarity in Catholic social teaching is sometimes used. He seemed to be saying that individuals working in just structures from below according to the traditional principle of subsidiarity is not enough. Governments also need to act from above in deliberate policy to work with individuals working from below in a reciprocal engagement which serves the common good. Governments and individuals meet in a plane of reciprocating effort, supporting each other in mutually reinforcing ways to serve the common good.

A complex interaction of individual and localised activity meets with high level government policy in a mutually engaging space – a reciprocation of effort where both support the other respective of their specific roles – a reciprocating subsidiarity. Under this approach to subsidiarity, higher forms of endeavour, like national parliaments, do not seek to defer to lower forces of individual activity but seek a compact where each find a common space of discourse. We may see more of this evolving concept of reciprocating subsidiarity from Francis, it seems part of his emerging discourse on economics to redress an individualistic approach to the principle of subsidiarity.

Evaluation

Francis is critical of neo-liberalism and in sceptical as to whether market-based mechanisms really can deal with the problems of climate change and social inequality. His innovative contribution is rather to call for a personal and political spirituality of economic asceticism. In essence, it is a less is more approach. In terms of political economy, he calls for a rethinking of the current paradigm by fostering a spirituality of asceticism. Francis claims that the throw-away culture of consumption (and production which is derivative of it) actually involves interference with the pursuit of the common good in economic terms seen as social inclusion or environmental safeguards. Francis' answer is that, for the sake of the Kingdom of God, for the sake of the common good, we should choose to constrain the appetite we aggressively display for personal consumption. It is a sort of Lenten penitential sermon, not just a private penitence for personal spiritual renewal, but recognition that this economic asceticism constitutes a collective *metanoia* from shared excesses of consumption that undermines the common good.

This is a strong call for social engagement from a left of centre political perspective combining environment concerns with an appreciation of the need to combat poverty and a degraded economic order. However, this strong political message needs be balanced against the tone of his speech given to the US Congress. His approach of constructive engagement with the world economic superpower was sustained throughout the papal visit but always with a sense of challenge. We see a political economy from Francis that is left in tone but moderated to circumstances, a practical call for gospel values and Catholic social teaching to inspire policy in a clear progressive political manner but not a doctrinaire approach. While certainly a challenging message, critical of economic processes, there is no clear alignment of this approach with the Marxist elements often attributed to liberation theology. This is shown in his use of the notion of reciprocating subsidiarity. The individual and local communities have a role to play in dealing with climate change and economic inequality implicated with it. Governments also have a role to play in their own spheres. Rather than a principle which brings conflict between the less aggregated and more highly aggregated forms of political and economic life, the two can and must act in unity, in a mutually reinforcing dialogue of reciprocating engagement – a reconciliation from below and above – meeting in a united shared voice for reform.

A Message to Governments – An Australian Case Study

While Francis' thought on political economy is relevant to all countries, in an Australian context, the first observation that can be made is the divergence between the approach Francis has taken to the principle of subsidiarity and the usages of the notion by the Australian Government *Commission of Audit Report* (2014) and in the language deployed by some conservative politicians. In the *Commission of Audit Report* for the new Coalition Government the principle of subsidiarity was a major theme. In essence, a philosophical view of political liberalism was presented that states that the Government should not seek to do for individuals what they can do for themselves. This was taken up by the Abbott Government in political rhetoric. Francis' reflections on this issue are, however, much more considered. His notion of reciprocating subsidiarity is not individualistic and his reflections in both *Evangelii Gaudium* and *Laudato Si'* clearly reject the philosophy of political liberalism in favour of his 'less is more' approach.

Whether or not the 'less is more' moral counsel of Francis is able to be deployed in a widespread fashion to change economic behavior is a book still to be written. Many economists will take tickets in a list of speakers in rebuttal. What is in fact at stake is a new approach to the moral theology of economics and such a work exceeds the scope of this essay. However, we can note that the economic asceticism of

Francis stands in contrast to the current rhetoric of 'jobs and growth' in the Australian political economy. For Francis, this seems to more of the same 'trickle down' approach – whereby the pursuit of merely economic gains for individuals misses the point that such economistic goals are implicated with the collective moral degradation present in a consumerist culture, and deploy a rhetoric which is not necessarily aligned with the pursuit of the common good in any sophisticated manner.

If we accept this line of economic reasoning from Pope Francis, we can identify one contemporary topic in policy that is at the centre of the political debate in Australia which his theology of economics speaks to. This policy is the extension of the *Goods and Services Tax* (GST). The GST was created by agreement of the States and Territories, with the support of Commonwealth Government legislation, to allow the Australian Tax Office to collect 10% of value of many transactions in Australian commerce, with credits for GST paid in the production chain so that it is only applied once. It excludes many things especially fresh food, health and education, some other government services and financial services. The revenue the Commonwealth provides to the States and Territories redresses in significant part the fiscal imbalance between the Commonwealth and the other jurisdictions and provides funds for service delivery most notably in health and education. While inherently regressive (all indirect taxes are imposed irrespective of the capacity to pay in income terms), the social expenditure it provides for can be very progressive if the services it funds are enjoyed proportionately more by persons on lower incomes.

Any student of Catholic social teaching, or any public theologian in the Christian tradition, knows that the body of thought which constitutes Christian reflection on economic and social policy matters is limited in what it can say on specific matters of public policy. Public theology is an evolving engagement with the world from a religious viewpoint. It presents a broad framework of evaluation based on a stated narrative and anthropology. For the Christian theologian, it is an anthropology informed by Christian revelation and arguably by elements of natural law. It is a hermeneutical process, an organic engagement of Christian minds informed by theology and lived Christian praxis that seeks to apply its core values and lived pastoral experience to the constantly changing dynamic of contemporary life in the here and now of our social, political and economic reality.

The question of the approach of a public theologian to tax policy highlights these constraints a *fortiori*. There are many more potential tax reforms than there are potential tax commentators. There are many more models of a specific tax reform programs than there are specific tax reform proposals. The author, who is a professional tax modeller, operates in this surreal world of grand theoretical calculations. It is a highly technical field – neurosurgery economist style. The public theologian engaged in the tax debate cannot claim that his recommendations carry with them any theological imperative. The outcomes of the model are contingent on a legion of contingencies and in the end the Christian tax economist can but put an argument among other arguments without claim to any special insight and certainly no theological warrants for any specific proposals. To do otherwise would be rendering to Caesar what is Caesar's without rendering to God what is God's. For divine revelation does not dictate tax policy in Australia in any strong sense at all. There is, however, something that a public theologian engaging in tax policy can do. He or she can identify broad themes and currents of contemporary theological debate and seek to use them to guide a policy program which serves the common good. We can apply Francis' approach to economic asceticism to the Australian tax debate. If as Francis argues, our tendency to indulge in personal consumption in the developed world leads to a throw-away culture of consumerism leading to social exclusion and environmental degradation in the whole world, the efforts to constrain this consumption oriented culture in the developed world are to be supported.

Extending the GST, by either increasing the base that is taxed (like including fresh food), or increasing the tax rate will act to ameliorate this culture of consumerism. Consumption is taxed and the monies raised fund progressive social expenditure. The culture of consumption is not destroyed, but the vice (in Francis' perspective) is taxed and the benefits are directed towards social programs. In this sense an expansion of the GST revenue stream in Australia seems to accord with Francis' call to an economic asceticism in our consumption choices.

Virtue is made of vice and the structural perversity he identifies in economic process is in part reversed. Taxes on consumption help to redirect consumption from purely personal goals towards social goals of redressing economic disadvantage. It is my reading of the emerging approach of Francis to economics that it supports an increase in the GST revenue take, as being aligned with pursuit of the common good in Australia.

Conclusion

Francis is challenging governments like Australia to adopt effective climate change policies reflecting the influence of environmental degradation on poverty. Linking explicitly the spirituality of St Francis to the words of the Australian bishops in *Laudato Si'* he says:

> In calling to mind the figure of Saint Francis of Assisi, we come to realise that a healthy relationship with creation is one dimension of overall personal conversion, which entails the recognition of our errors, sins, faults and failures, and leads to heartfelt repentance and desire to change. The Australian bishops spoke of the importance of such conversion for achieving reconciliation with creation: 'To achieve such reconciliation, we must examine our lives and acknowledge the ways in which we have harmed God's creation through our actions and our failure to act. We need to experience a conversion or change of heart' (LS, 218).

So Australian Catholic theologians, and economists engaging practical theology in dialogue with economics, now have a well-defined brief. That brief is to engage with Francis' emerging moral theology of economics and apply this to policy debate in this nation. If we follow Francis' reasoning, these challenges are not only to be taken up in the environmental agenda, but also in the area of social inclusion. Approaches to tax policy are a key part of this social inclusion agenda. Francis' call for an option for an economic asceticism to serve the common good presents challenges for public theology in Australia, in fact rather radical challenges. A serious reflection on Francis' 'less is more' or 'more is less' theology of economics, might well led Christian economists towards strong policy positions on issues at the heart of economic debates. In fact, it seems that this is exactly what he is calling us to do.

Chapter Eight

Discerning the Place for the Prophetic Voice and Pragmatic Co-operation of the Churches in the Great Moral Questions of the Age

Frank Brennan

I take heart from the declaration of the Second Vatican Council in its decree on ecumenism: 'All those justified by faith through baptism are incorporated into Christ. They therefore have a right to be honoured by the title of Christian, and are properly regarded as brothers and sisters in the Lord by the sons and daughters of the Catholic Church'.[1] So I greet you as brothers and sisters in the Lord.

Might I assure those of you from the smaller countries in Oceania that we Australians are learning a new humility in the wake of our now constant losses to New Zealand in the Rugby World Cup and our increasing reliance on players coming from other countries in Oceania to add gravitas to the Wallaby scrum and to enhance the speed of its backline. And there is absolutely no risk of us Australians taking the high moral ground given the way we have prostituted our aid program and undermined nation building in the Pacific simply so as to find a place to dump asylum seekers who have come to our shores. We welcome you to a country which has exploited its status as a wealthy island nation continent for short term political gain playing on the fears of an isolationist public.

Thirty years ago next month, I was ordained priest in St Stephen's Cathedral Brisbane. I was privileged to have the Catholic bishops of Queensland joined on the sanctuary by the Primate of the Anglican Church and the Moderator of the Uniting Church in Queensland.

---

[1] Vatican II, *Unitatis Redintegratio*, (1964), 'Decree on Ecumenism', 3.

Archbishops John Grindrod and Frank Rush had worked together in the country diocese of Rockhampton before going to Brisbane. John then became Primate of Anglican Church and Frank was President of the Australian Catholic Bishops Conference. I worked with them and Doug Brandon, the Uniting Church moderator, in our joint commitment to improving the lives of Aborigines and Torres Strait Islanders during some testing political times including the Commonwealth Games held in Brisbane in 1982. We sometimes came into conflict with the native New Zealander Sir Joh Bjelke Petersen who was the colourful premier of Queensland. When it came time for my ordination, it seemed only natural and appropriate that the leaders of the three major Churches in Queensland pray together that the Spirit come upon me in priestly service. It was by doing something co-operative together for the cause of justice that we found our way clear to worship together and that we wanted to pray together in the most formal of liturgical contexts. But for our joint endeavour in the public square for justice, there is no way that we would have all prayed together on that sanctuary that night in Brisbane.

In recent years, our ecumenical efforts have grown a little stale, I daresay. I well recall staying with Bishop John Bathersby over twenty years ago when he was Catholic bishop of Cairns. Coming down to breakfast one morning, I asked what was on his agenda for the day. He lamented that he had to attend a meeting of the Ministers Fraternal. I exuded that such ecumenical activity was very worthwhile. He responded, 'But they want me to sign a letter opposing the building of a casino.' I opined that this was a worthy social protest. He scratched his bald pate complaining, 'But it's a bit hard when your old man was an SP bookie.' We need worthy causes that fire our passion to bring us together ecumenically.

In recent years, no longer isolated in our confessional ghettos, all of us have had to become more engaged in giving an account of our hope to those who do not share our faith tradition or even our faith. Since 11 September 2001, we are all aware of the need to engage with Muslims. The rising tide of secularism demands that we engage in the public square in a way which is comprehensible and appealing to those of all faiths and none. The crisis of child sexual abuse in our societies, from which the churches are by no means exempt, has required that our institutional procedures be more transparent and that we learn from the ways of the world in exercising power openly and justly. This means we have to restructure some of our church arrangements so that power is exercised accountably and transparently. All of us who have positions of influence and power in institutional churches need to be attentive to the voices of those who have suffered within our institutions. Only yesterday, Julie Stewart, a victim of sexual abuse by a Catholic priest gave evidence in the case study into the Melbourne Catholic Archdiocese being conducted by the Australian Royal Commission into Institutional Responses to Child Sexual Abuse. Making her opening statement, she concluded with these words (Transcript 13253-4):

> I still cry for the little girl I once was. The little girl that never got to be a normal little girl, doing all the things that little girls should do. The little girl who always just wanted to fit in, but always felt like a weirdo, like a problem. Nothing can ever give that back to me. It is a life sentence, and every day I make a choice to keep going.
> It is important to me to tell my story now, because I want peace for myself. I want peace for Mr Sleeman [the school principal who fought to have the dreadful abuser Fr Searson dismissed]. I've got kids and I want to be a voice. I want people to know that this happened. I'm not ashamed anymore, and I no longer blame myself. I will no longer be a victim. My name is Julie Stewart.

We need to express our gratitude as well as our sorrow to those like Julie Stewart who have courageously come forward helping us all to understand, and reminding us what we truly profess in the name of Christ.

In the wake of recent terrorist attacks in Beirut, Paris and Mali, it is timely to revisit Pope Benedict's confronting Regensberg address, particularly the Christian emperor's observation to his Muslim interlocutor: 'Faith is born of the soul, not the body. Whoever would lead someone to faith needs the ability to speak well and to reason properly, without violence and threats.' Whether our enterprise be interfaith dialogue, ecumenical relations, or engagement with the state and society in the public square, there is no substitute for speaking well and reasoning properly.

The good speaker knows their audience and appeals to their cultural predispositions and historical consciousness as did Pope Francis when appearing recently at the US Congress. Wherever we speak in Oceania, we need to be immersed in the local cultures and situation. Think only of the brilliance of Francis during his address to the US Congress quoting four noted Americans, two of whom were not Catholic, one of the Catholics being a woman who had an abortion and was a single mum, and the other Catholic a monk who had an affair, a peace activist who was silenced by his superiors. The four were Abraham Lincoln, Martin Luther King, Dorothy Day and Thomas Merton. Francis commenced his address, going in the audience's door with the words:

> I am most grateful for your invitation to address this Joint Session of Congress in 'the land of the free and the home of the brave'. I would like to think that the reason for this is that I too am a son of this great continent, from which we have all received so much and toward which we share a common responsibility.

He praised the American people for their culture and their history despites its many blemishes:

> A nation can be considered great when it defends liberty as Lincoln did, when it fosters a culture which enables people to 'dream' of full rights for all their brothers and sisters, as Martin Luther King sought to do; when it strives for justice and the cause of the oppressed, as Dorothy Day did by her tireless work, the fruit of a faith which becomes dialogue and sows peace in the contemplative style of Thomas Merton.

The prophetic voice has more chance of being heard when it resonates not with jingoistic nationalism but when it accords with the audience's sense of their abiding values and salvation history marked out on their land and in their time.

The acute thinker knows that their interlocutors speak on many levels, at times invoking religious and philosophical edicts, and at other times applying those edicts to the situation at hand. The interpretation of the edicts requires attention, as when our Australian ex-prime minister Tony Abbott delivering the Margaret Thatcher oration says, 'Justice tempered by mercy is an exacting ideal as too much mercy for some necessarily undermines justice for all.' Mercy for one never undermines justice for others. We can be committed to providing each their due, providing justice for all, while then being able to offer mercy only to some. Even if mercy be selectively shown, an inequitable distribution of mercy does not undermine justice for all. I can be committed to justice for all and then to mercy only for those proximate to me. So too a government or a group.

In his Thatcher Oration, Tony Abbott eloquently said: 'Implicitly or explicitly, the imperative to 'love your neighbour as you love yourself' is at the heart of every Western polity. It expresses itself in laws protecting workers, in strong social security safety nets, and in the readiness to take in refugees. It's what makes us decent and humane countries as well as prosperous ones'. But then he went badly off the rails with his observation that 'right now – this wholesome instinct is leading much of Europe into catastrophic error.' The gospel imperative of love of neighbour is not just an instinct; it is an injunction by our Lord and Saviour. Those of us who exercise public office know that we will be called upon to discharge a public trust which often fails to extend love to all who are our neighbour. Each of us must ultimately give an account of ourselves, not just to the electorate for the exercise of the public trust but to our Lord and Saviour for the conduct of our lives, including public service.

The application of the edicts requires scrutiny as when Mr Abbott applying the edict of justice and mercy fails to distinguish the situations of boat people headed for Australia and those headed for Europe. He told his British Tory audience: 'So it's good that Europe has now deployed naval vessels to intercept people smuggling boats in the Mediterranean – but as long as they're taking passengers aboard rather than turning boats around and sending them back, it's a facilitator rather than a deterrent'. Writing in this week's *Spectator*, he acknowledges that there are two different situations at play in the waters off Europe: 'For a couple of years now, thousands of people a month have been coming by boat from Libya to Italy; and over the past few months, new routes have opened by land from Turkey and by sea to Greece'. The French Ambassador Christophe Lecourtier when speaking on the ABC *Q&A* discredited completely the Abbott comparison and identification of the Australian and European situations when he observed politely, 'But, you know, you just have to look at what is the geography and also the geopolitical of Europe and it's not something you can do like that'.

Even if it be legal and safe to return boats to Indonesia when asylum seekers are not in direct flight from persecution in Indonesia, no one could in good conscience return Somalian and Eritrean asylum seekers on the Mediterranean to the transit country of Libya which is now a failed state. I would be so bold as to suggest that not even an Abbott government could have been elected in Australia with a commitment to return asylum seekers to Indonesia if Indonesia were a failed state unable to ensure compliance with the principle of non-refoulement.

Tony Abbott told his unknowing audience on the other side of the world, 'The immigration detention centres have all-but-closed'. If that were so, it would surely be time for Malcolm Turnbull, with support from Bill Shorten, to close them. What part of the 'all-but' can be justified as fulfilling any purpose at all, other than wanton cruelty in the name of political advantage? Now that the boats have stopped, immigration detention should be used only for health, security and identity checks and for holding, pending deportation. The detention centres on Nauru and Manus Island do not pass muster.

> The report of the expert panel led by Sir Angus Houston in August 2012 stated:
> The Panel is of the strong view that there are a range of conditions that need to be fulfilled for the safe and lawful turnback of boats carrying asylum seekers. The Panel does not believe those conditions currently exist, although they could at some stage in the future, in particular if appropriate regional and bilateral arrangements are in place.

I have accepted the decision of the Turnbull Government and Shorten Opposition to stop the boats provided two conditions are fulfilled: (1) an immediate assessment is made that no person on board is fleeing persecution *in* Indonesia; and (2) the boats can be turned back legally and safely. I would prefer that those intercepted were picked up and flown back to Indonesia safely and decently.

I would like to know what has happened to the boat that was intercepted off Christmas Island last week. Are the people who were on that boat safe? What has been done to them in our name? What are the new regional and bilateral arrangements that have been put in place since August 2012 which satisfied our military personnel last week that they were acting lawfully and honourably?

I do wish our Parliament would demand that the government make clear how such turnbacks are safe and lawful. After all, the Labor Opposition is saying that it will retain the option to turn back boats only where it is safe to do so. Is Labor satisfied that the boat which disappeared from sight just off Christmas Island was safely turned back? How would they know unless they asked? I wonder what Sir Angus thinks. On Monday afternoon, Senator Hanson Young asked the Attorney-General in the Senate: 'I would like to ask the minister if he can please explain the sighting of a boat just three days ago, when a refugee boat reportedly made it to within 200 metres of Christmas Island. Could the minister explain why this boat was there, how many people were on it and where it is now?' George Brandis, the Attorney-General, refused to answer, pleading that it was an operational matter. And the circus of Australian democracy and the so called rule of law moved on. We are not to be told, and it is all done in our name. It's revolting. Here in Australia, our church leaders have published fine and lofty statements about the rights and entitlements of asylum seekers. But where is their voice to be heard when a boatload of hapless souls arrives only to be towed into oblivion? Where is the church agency with the mandate to follow up on the fine church statements, calling our elected leaders to account?

Religious leaders in the public square of the pluralist, democratic society founded on the rule of law are charged with being prophetic, appealing to the better nature and the nobler aspirations of the public, drawing unapologetically on the strengths of their own religious tradition, while being pragmatic and sufficiently respectful of those charged with the public trust of exercising the power of the state in the name of the people.

Living and working in societies where there is no philosophical agreement about the basis for, or the limits of, state power interfering with personal autonomy, and being members of faith communities and churches without any theological consensus about the basis of human rights and human dignity (whether inherent or attributed), how can we authentically and usefully contribute to the development of laws and public policies which enhance human flourishing, and perhaps even counsel a social striving for perfection? This is a question which confronts all religious leaders in a pluralistic democratic society. It may be an even more pressing question for the citizen of faith who occupies a position of public trust, whether as legislator, judge or administrator. What can we do? What should we do? What should we forbear from doing, regardless of our personal convictions, when discharging that public trust? What can we learn from each other coming from countries with diverse constitutional arrangements about how best to resolve disputes about law and policy relating to contested moral questions? How can the human rights actor best speak out for those suffering, whilst maintaining the agency of those suffering?

Those of us who profess to be Christian living behind secure national borders buttressed by wealth and the rule of law being shared only by the citizenry have been wrestling with the gospel imperatives of justice and compassion expressed in the parables of Jesus such as the parable of the Good Samaritan. The Oxford academic John Finnis reminds us that 'neither atheism nor radical agnosticism is entitled to be treated as the "default" position in public reason, deliberation and decisions. Those who say or assume that there is a default position and that it is secular in those senses (atheism or agnosticism about atheism) owe us an argument that engages with and defeats the best arguments for divine causality.'[2] Though it might be prudent and strategic to suggest that religious accommodationists carry the onus of persuasion in a public square with a secularist prejudice, might there not be a case

---

[2] John Finnis, *Religion and Public Reasons* (Oxford: Oxford University Press, 2011) 45.

for arguing that the representatives of the more populist, majoritarian mindset in the public square need to be more accommodating of religious views? Think just of the absurd situation in Tasmania at the moment where it is suggested that the Catholic bishops may have a case to answer under the state's anti-discrimination law because they have had the temerity to inform their faithful about the church's traditional teaching on marriage.

Finnis, a Catholic but making a point equally applicable to all faith communities, says, 'Outside the Church, it is widely assumed and asserted that any proposition which the Catholic Church in fact proposes for acceptance is, by virtue of that fact, a "religious" (not a philosophical, scientific, or rationally grounded and compelling proposition), and is a proposition which Catholics hold only as a matter of faith and therefore cannot be authentically willing to defend as a matter of natural reason.'[3] For Finnis, much of what John Rawls in his *Political Liberalism* describes as public reason can be equated with natural reason. Whereas Rawls would rely on an overlapping consensus not wanting to press for objective reality of right and wrong, Finnis would contest that the only content of an overlapping consensus would be that which can be objectively known through natural reason.

Discourse in the public square is a two-way street. Thus, for example, there is a place for Pope Francis at Lampedusa to be prophetically declaiming the moral turpitude of present European state practices in relation to the rescue of asylum seekers in the Mediterranean Sea. There is a place for the Australian church leaders to be prophetically declaiming the moral turpitude of present state practices towards asylum seekers on Christmas Island, Nauru and Manus Island. There is a place for church leaders drawing on their religious tradition trying to call political leaders and the public back to values, policies and laws which resonate more with the tenets of religious faith.

The migration and asylum debate is one debate in which the voice of community leaders, and not just lawyers, needs to be heeded and in which we need to have due regard for political deliberation. It is one of those debates requiring an attentiveness to the still, small voice of conscience. Often, nowadays, the best amplifiers of that

---
[3] Finnis, (2011), 114-5.

voice are not the religious leaders but the poets, novelists and folk singers. In Australia, one of our finest novelists Tim Winton made a rare appearance on the public stage on Palm Sunday 2015, dissenting from Australia's refugee policy. Conceding that he was 'no expert, no politician', and expressing no envy of 'those who make the decisions in these matters, those who've sought and gained the power to make decisions in this matter', he declared, 'But I know when something's wrong. And what my country is doing is wrong.'[4] He lamented:

> We're losing our way. We have hardened our hearts. I fear we have devalued the currency of mercy. Children have asked for bread and we gave them stones. So turn back. I beg you. For the children's sake. For the sake of this nation's spirit. Raise us back up to our best selves. Turn back while there's still time.

The distillation of the prophetic message is often assisted by ecumenical critiques by those outside the circle of church hierarchy and tradition, as for example when Rowan Williams writes a reflection on Pope Francis' encyclical *Laudato Si*. The coherence of the pragmatic engagement is enhanced when ecumenical discernment and joint action results in a message being communicated which is not dependent on only one church tradition or authority.

My appreciation of *Laudato Si* has been enhanced by Rowan Williams' observation:

> If we can lift our heads from the trenches of contemporary media-driven controversy, what we are being offered in this encyclical is, in the very fullest sense, a theology of liberation, drawing our minds and hearts toward a converted culture that is neither what T. S. Eliot called 'ringing the bell backwards,' pining for a lost social order and a lost form or style of authority, nor a religiously inflected liberalism, but a genuinely ecclesial vision. The pope's cultural revolution is about restored relationship with the creation we belong with and the creator who made us to share his bliss in communion; it is about the unbreakable links between contemplation, Eucharist, justice,

---

[4] See http://www.watoday.com.au/comment/tim-wintons-palm-sunday-plea-start-thesoul searching-australia-20150329-1ma5so.html.

and social transformation. It constitutes a major contribution to the ongoing unfolding of a body of coherent social teaching, and a worthy expansion and application of the deeply impressive doctrinal syntheses of Pope Benedict's major encyclicals.

And yes it does make a difference to me that these words are uttered by an Anglican theologian who had been Archbishop of Canterbury rather than by a Catholic who may still be awaiting further promotion within the hierarchy enjoying the favour of the present Holy Father.

If those of us from diverse Christian traditions cannot agree on the moral basis for arguments about inequality, climate change, same sex marriage or euthanasia, we cannot expect our politicians to take our distinctive religious arguments as much more than quaint observations from the sidelines by those who bear no responsibility for exercising power which impacts on the citizenry, the marginalised and the common good. Respectful ecumenical dialogue is an essential pre-condition for any meaningful engagement by church leaders in the public square. But you could be forgiven for thinking it is the step most often overlooked with the result that even the most resourced church campaign for or against an issue is perceived and caricatured as special pleading by a religious sect. Good ecumenical relations, ecumenical co-operation on projects, and respectful, informed ecumenical critique are indispensable tools for any faith-based engagement on the great moral questions of the age.

Professor Margaret Somerville who directs the Center for Law, Ethics and Medicine at McGill University in Montreal has just published a book of essays entitled *Bird on the Ethics Wire: Battles About Values in the Culture Wars*.[5] Somerville has been a long time participant in the public square involved in debates on euthanasia, stem cell research and same sex marriage. She says 'that we can no longer assume, as we once could, that we all share more or less the same fundamental values. If society was ever that homogenous, those days are long gone.'[6] She sees a 'crisis of conflict between respect for individual autonomy and protection of the common good' with too much emphasis on individual autonomy.

---

[5] Margaret Somerville, *Bird on the Ethics Wire: Battles About Values in the Culture Wars*, (McGill-Queens University Press, 2015).
[6] Somerville, (2015), xiii.

You don't necessarily have to be religious to think that doctors should do no harm, that patients are free to forego futile or burdensome treatment, and that palliative care be utilised to relieve pain. Suicide will occur from time to time, but why the need to enact laws conferring medical legitimation and increasing its likelihood? I readily concede that in jurisdictions like the US state of Oregon, to date, they have maintained a bright line between euthanasia and physician assisted suicide – but it's a line which has been dimmed by the Canadian Supreme Court's bright spotlight of autonomy recently illuminated in their 2015 *Carter* decision. It's a line which would be extinguished were the Canadian judicial thinking to take hold elsewhere. I do worry about the slippery slope for vulnerable patients who might think they have no option but taking their own lives. I remain committed to the simple Hippocratic Oath, 'Do no harm.' Don't take life. Care for the dying by relieving their suffering. And that's not just because I'm Catholic.

As we wrestle with these issues, maintaining the balance between autonomy and the common good, we need to maintain what Pope John Paul II called 'a convinced and pondered trust in the heritage of virtues and values handed down by our forebears'. Those of us with religiously informed ideas about the common good and human dignity need to be active participants in the intellectual and cultural dialogue which is 'essential to the discovery of truth in a historically conscious world'[7]. Any church interventions should, as the US Jesuit ethicist David Hollenbach says, be 'carefully cast as documents that (seek) to persuade rather than coerce'.[8]

It will be some time before we come back to level ground on contested issues such as euthanasia. While welcoming a prosecutorial policy which does not threaten the compassion for, or the dignity of, those who assist invulnerable and competent, horrifically disabled persons, we should continue to have a community care and a state concern for those many others who can be dissuaded from suicide with society's legitimate concern and commitment to kill the pain and relieve the existential angst without killing the person, and leaving others to

---

[7] David Hollenbach, *The Global Face of Public Faith*, (Georgetown University Press, 2003), 142.
[8] Hollenbach, (2003), 144.

carry the burden of yet more suicides. We need to consider the dignity and integrity of those suffering dementia or Alzheimer's Disease, no longer able to communicate free, informed decisions, let alone to reverse those decisions even should they so wish. The law needs to have a care for the dignity of all these persons, equally. Facilitating assistance with suicide for any autonomous person who wants it is not the way to enhance the dignity of those radically questioning the utility or worth of life that 'you'll feel safe and cared-for in a community where everyone supports each other'. We need to maintain our toehold on the slippery slope no matter what the superficial appeal of the judicial reasoning that we can extend autonomy, non-discrimination and individual human rights universally, all the way down to the valley of death.

I had the opportunity to be on the other side of the table discerning the place for the prophetic voice and pragmatic co-operation of the Churches in 2009 when chairing the National Human Rights Consultation for the Rudd government. The various spokespersons for the three majority Christian denominations put a variety of viewpoints to my committee about the desirability of a federal *Human Rights Act*. The Australian Catholic Bishops Conference submitted:

> In considering the question raised by the terms of reference of the National Human Rights Consultation, it is noted that much discussion has been about whether or not there should be a Charter of Rights. On that particular issue, the ACBC does not take a particular stand at this stage.

In their submission, the Australian Catholic Bishops Conference restated: 'The Australian Catholic Bishops Conference does not have a position as to whether or not there should be a Charter of Rights.'

The Anglican General Synod submitted:

> We support the enactment of human rights legislation because this has the potential to have a beneficial effect on government policy and the legislation and administration, which give effect to that policy. Legislators and administrators will be compelled by such legislation to consider the impact of their decisions on

all Australians, especially the most vulnerable. Further, the existence of human rights legislation could encourage greater understanding of human rights in the community.

But then again, the Standing Committee of the Synod of the Anglican Church Diocese of Sydney submitted:

> We consider that the adoption of a Federal charter of rights would, at best, make little difference to the protection of human rights and may, at worst, undermine the protection of human rights in Australia.

The Uniting Church National Assembly submitted:

> The Uniting Church believes that a *Human Rights Act*, operating within Australia's system of open and democratic government, will provide greater protection for fundamental rights and freedoms, promote dignity, address disadvantage and exclusion, and help to create a 'human rights culture' in Australia. Furthermore, it will serve to promote Australia's commitment to human rights in the Asia-Pacific and globally, and formalise the current Government's commitment to the United Nations by those putting it into effect.

As if all that was not confusing enough, in contradistinction to the Australian Catholic Bishops Conference which sat on the fence, the Archdiocese of Sydney submitted:

> There are initiatives which could be taken to better protect and promote human rights in Australia, but there are serious reasons for doubting that a statutory charter of rights is the best way of doing this.

This submission followed upon Cardinal Pell's address the previous year when he stated his opposition to a charter of rights in any form. He told the Brisbane Institute:

> The suspicion of majority — that is, parliamentary — rule, the preference for judicial, as opposed to political, determination of fundamental questions, the unacceptable transfer of

responsibility from the parliament to the courts, and the unspoken assumptions which inform not only these tendencies but the particular social and political agenda which a bill of rights is intended to implement, are some of the critical problems with the proposals for a bill or charter of rights. These problems are compounded by confusion over the foundations of human rights, freedom and truth.

Moving beyond the neutral position of the Australian Catholic Bishops Conference, the Catholic Archdioceses of Sydney and Melbourne then co-operated in activities with the Australian Christian Lobby (ACL) during the inquiry. The Lobby was vigorously opposed to a *Human Rights Act* in any form. The then Anglican Archbishop of Sydney, Peter Jensen, joined forces with other church leaders opposed to a Charter in any form, despite the submission from the Anglican General Synod supporting a Charter. For me and my committee members, it was difficult to get a handle on just who the ACL represented.

Once church leaders join forces with a group such as the ACL, it is then difficult to know how to assess the earlier formal statements of the church leaders which may not be fully consistent with the Lobby's implacable opposition to a measure such as a *Human Rights Act*.

Given the diversity of opinion expressed by the ACBC and the Catholic Archdiocese of Sydney, as well as the diversity of opinion between the Anglican General Synod and their Sydney Archbishop, and given the ambiguous role and relationship between the ACL and some church leaders, it became too complex a task to try and represent in the report the viewpoint of the various churches on a *Human Rights Act*. Thus we omitted all reference to same. I daresay this will become a common response by public inquiries which doubt the public's interest in investigating the complex arrangements now in place for church leaders to express views under various guises. After our report was published, one Church leader wrote to me saying:

> The decision to exclude different views expressed by the churches seems to suggest that on social issues, if the churches cannot speak in one voice, they will not be given a say at all.

You clearly foreshadow that this is what can be expected from similar sorts of public inquiries in the future. All this would do, if it were to happen, is to call into question the good faith of those conducting such 'consultations'.

The impugning of the standing of the consultation need not be the only consequence; in fact it might not be one of the consequences at all. One consequence might be the churches condemning themselves to irrelevance.

Though sceptical about the more overblown claims of human rights advocates, I became convinced as our committee criss-crossed the country that the language and architecture of human rights are necessary for our ongoing commitment to recognise the inherent human dignity of every person, giving them their due and ensuring that the State does not violate their human freedom.

If those of us from diverse Christian traditions cannot agree on the moral basis for arguments about inequality, climate change, same sex marriage or euthanasia, we cannot expect our politicians to take our distinctive religious arguments as much more than quaint observations from the sidelines by those who bear no responsibility for exercising power which impacts on the citizenry, the marginalised and the common good.

Religious leaders in the public square of the pluralist, democratic society founded on the rule of law are charged with being prophetic, appealing to the better nature and the nobler aspirations of the public while being pragmatic and sufficiently respectful of those charged with the public trust of exercising the power of the state in the name of the people. How do we ensure that the inherent dignity of the stranger is part of the calculus deciding what is fair and appropriate? The unvisaed asylum seeker is often viewed as a person without inherent dignity. Their dignity is acquired only once they obtain a visa. On the edges of society, and at the beginning and end of the life cycle, the utilitarian sees no case for espousing or affirming the inherent dignity of all. Dignity is acquired and forfeited depending on where the person is in the cycle or in the society, depending on the balance of good and bad consequences for others in attributing dignity to that person.

The late Edmond Pellegrino who chaired the US President's Council on Bioethics once observed:

> Two contrary, but not necessarily contradictory, world views will dominate the discourse in our post-secular civilisation. Two images of human dignity compete for moral authority. One is the scientific, the other the religious. Neither is likely to capitulate to the other. Is a productive dialogue and dialectic between these two world views possible, and how is it to be conducted?

Extremists on both sides, militant atheists and intransigent dogmatists, insist there can be no common ground. More responsible proponents of both views hope for a productive dialogue and appeal to the necessity of a common ground in the public arena, even while metaphysical foundations remain disputed.[9]

We need to be more confident in the expression and living of our culture of faith if we as Christians are to contribute distinctively to our world. Such a task is not disheartening; it fires our passion and imagination as did the stranger that day on the road to Emmaus and that night at the table: 'Were not our hearts burning within us while he talked with us on the road and opened the Scriptures to us?'

Pope Francis went to Rome's principal Lutheran church on Sunday 8 November 2015. Benedict had done the same five years ago. And John Paul II had been there back in 1983. On arrival Francis presented the Lutherans with a gift - a chalice for celebration of the Eucharist.

A Lutheran who was married to a Catholic then asked him why she could not receive Communion when she attended Mass with her husband. Francis replied:

> As to your question, I will just respond with a question: how can I do (this) with my husband, so the Supper of the Lord can accompany on my journey? This is a problem to which each person must respond. But a friend who's a pastor told me: 'We believe the Lord is present there. He's present. You believe the Lord is present. What's the difference?' – Eh,

---

[9] Somerville, (2015), 115-6.

there are explanations and interpretations. Life is greater than explanations and interpretations. Always make reference to baptism: 'One faith, one baptism, one Lord', as St Paul tells us, and draw the consequences from that. I would never dare to give permission to do this because it's not my competence. One baptism, one Lord, one faith. Speak to the Lord and go forward. I dare say no more.

He's let the genie out of the bottle. Perhaps we are on the verge of being able to recognise each other in the breaking of the bread on the road to Emmaus.

None of us has all the answers as we struggle against eternal irrelevance – not even, dare I say it, the Holy Roman Catholic Church. The poet Emily Dickenson reminds us, 'The possible's slow fuse is lit by the imagination.' As we look at the faces of others, including perfect strangers to us and our traditions, turned towards God, let us do things together committed to the inherent dignity of all persons, and let us embrace the multi-faceted mystery of God reflected in the diverse expression on those myriad faces turned towards God in churches, mosques, synagogues, crowded streets and open fields this night.

In 1985, I was walking along the beach at Mapoon on the west coast of Cape York in far north Queensland and saw the largest mango tree I had ever seen. Mapoon had been established as a Presbyterian Aboriginal mission in the nineteenth century. Under the tree I saw Jean Jimmy who had just become a great great grandmother. As ever she was rolling a cigarette. I admired the tree and asked if the missionaries had planted it. 'No', she replied, 'I planted this tree. I am very blessed to sit under the shade of this tree and to see it bearing fruit.'

As we sit under the shade of the mango tree each of us has planted contemplating the bread and wine, may we commit ourselves afresh to justice, reconciliation and human rights for all, confident that if we work at that together we will naturally pray, eat and drink together helping even the secular, populist utilitarians in our midst to stave off eternal irrelevance. And let's stick up for each other when attacked by those whose power base is threatened by the prophetic utterance. In 2005 when being feted with an honorary doctorate at the Melbourne

College of Divinity, Peter Carnley, one time primate of the Anglican Church in Australia observed, 'In the course of the little spat I had last year with (his fellow Anglicans) Messrs Howard and Downer (over the Iraq War and the contested causes of the Bali bombing), I was not conscious of receiving much concrete support from within my own church. The person who most fearlessly and vocally came to my support was Fr Frank Brennan SJ. This signals the truth that it is a fact of life these days that we often find our most supportive kindred spirits across the denominational divide, in Churches other than our own.'

When I first studied at Georgetown University Law School twenty years ago, one of my mentors was Fr Ladislas Orsy SJ. While holding the Gasson Chair at Boston College in 2014-2015, I had the opportunity to meet again with Las. Now in his 90s, he gave me a copy of his last published article entitled, 'The Divine Dignity of Human Persons in *Dignitatis Humanae*'.[10] It is Las's reaffirmation that Vatican II is the Catholic Church's affirmation of belief in the human person who has a conscience. Orsy is a great advocate for true human freedom as the precondition for human flourishing and the thriving of any society buttressed by the rule of law. He espouses individual freedom:

> Persons are free internally when their spirit in its deliberations, decisions, and actions is independent, when it is not imposed or hampered by an outside agent or by their own unruly passions. They are free externally when no outside power coerces them physically or sets up obstacles for their intended actions.[11]

While being a great advocate of human freedom and individual virtue, Orsy makes no claims to human infallibility. He observes, 'Integrity does not guarantee the truth of a judgment or the prudence of an intended action. For that it must rely on critical intelligence. The task of conscience is not to create infallible knowledge or unfailing wisdom but to keep a person faithful to his or her honestly acquired conviction.'[12] Having had a year away from the Australian public square, I had the time and space to ponder what Las would call the

---

[10] Ladislas Orsy, 'The Divine Dignity of Human Persons in *Dignitatis Humanae*' (*Theological Studies* 2014, Vol 75(1) 8-22).
[11] Orsy, (2014), *Theological Studies* 17.
[12] Orsy, (2014), *Theological Studies* 16.

grace of integrity, knowing that I was returning to a church scene and a public square which is often very sterile, bereft, and unanchored. All any of us religious believers can bring to the public square is our integrity and inner freedom, together with our simple faith that God is with us giving us hope as we go forward. After a lifetime of engagement in the Church and the public square, Orsy writes:

> Persons have integrity when their inner being is transfused by harmony; when their decisions and actions flow from their honest judgment; when they faithfully pursue the values that they comprehend as means to their perfection. In contrast, they lose their integrity when their volitions and operations are divorced from their vision. Should such a disaster happen, the persons in question become traitors to themselves. Their inner world shatters; it becomes fragmented.

Integrity, however, does not mean that the individual judgments held by persons of integrity are by that fact alone correct and critically unassailable. Quite the opposite: their convictions must be open to critical examination and verification.[13]

I have returned to Australia open to dialogue with anybody, happy to have my convictions questioned and verified, and free on my part to question especially those who exercise authority. Without freedom and integrity, there is nothing any of us can contribute to the swirling mess of institutions which have lost public confidence, including the hierarchical church and the materialistic secularist public square which is marred by short term political conniving, an increasingly isolated and sterile jurisprudence, and a titillating shallow media. We are called into trusting, honest, self-disclosing dialogue with those seeking human flourishing for all, regardless of the utterances and strategies of those who enjoy short term power and success. We need to proclaim in comprehensible language and with incarnated symbolism the breaking in of the kingdom of God here and now. And we need to do this, grounded in our social reality, alert to the claims of those who are marginalised and suffering ongoing injustice.

---

[13] Orsy, (2014), *Theological Studies* 15.

When the going gets tough and the way ahead is not clear, we Church people can take to heart the observation by Morris West:

> The pronouncements of religious leaders will carry more weight, will be seen as more relevant if they are delivered in the visible context of a truly pastoral function, which is the mediation of the mystery of creation; the paradox of the silent Godhead and suffering humanity.

That's what Pope Francis has been doing so well of late. At all times in the public domain, whether in dialogue with government about social policy or in giving a public account of church perspectives, we who speak with a Church mantle must speak with the voice of public reason. Therein lies the tension. Without trust between those whose consciences differ, we will not scale the heights of the silence of the Godhead nor plumb the depths of the suffering of humanity; we will have failed to incarnate the mystery of God here among us. This mystery is to be embraced in the inner sanctuary of conscience where God's voice echoes within, to be enfleshed in the relationships we share as the people of God, and to be proclaimed in our calls for justice in the public domain.

It is only together, and through dialogue, that we will discern the place for the prophetic voice and pragmatic co-operation of our Churches in the great moral questions of the age.

www.ingramcontent.com/pod-product-compliance
Lightning Source LLC
Chambersburg PA
CBHW051947290426
44110CB00015B/2147